REAL ROLE MODELS

Real Role Models

SUCCESSFUL AFRICAN AMERICANS BEYOND POP CULTURE

JOAH SPEARMAN & LOUIS HARRISON, JR., PHD

University of Texas Press   *Austin*

Requests for permission to reproduce material from this work
should be sent to:
  Permissions
  University of Texas Press
  P.O. Box 7819
  Austin, TX 78713-7819
  www.utexas.edu/utpress/about/bpermission.html

⊚ The paper used in this book meets the minimum requirements
of ANSI/NISO Z39.48-1992 (R1997) (Permanence of Paper).

LIBRARY OF CONGRESS CATALOGING-IN-PUBLICATION DATA
Spearman, Joah, 1983–
Real role models : Successful African Americans beyond pop
culture / Joah Spearman and Louis Harrison, Jr. — 1st ed.
        p.   cm.
ISBN 978-0-292-72301-6 (cloth : alk. paper)
ISBN 978-0-292-71832-6 (pbk. : alk. paper)
   1. African Americans—Biography.   2. Role models—United
States—Biography.   3. Successful people—United States—
Biography.   4. African American professional employees—United
States—Biography.   5. African American leadership.   I. Harrison,
Louis, 1955– II. Title.
E185.96.S684   2010
920.009296073—dc22

                                                2009028224

To our mothers — our real role models and so much more

Contents

PART THREE: HOW THEY DO IT

Preface

While Dr. Martin Luther King, Jr.'s life was ended far too soon, no assassin could shoot down his legacy, his dream, or, most of all, his desire for a day when we all would be judged by the content of our character rather than the color of our skin. The election of Barack Obama as the nation's first black president is a testament to that. Dr. King envisioned an America without racism and prejudice, but also without inequality. He often spoke of this ideal: a nation where every young black boy and girl, like their white counterparts, would grow up with ample opportunities to become successful people. We now know that holding even the world's most powerful job is within our reach if we set our minds to it.

This book grabs ahold of Dr. King's dream and channels that positive energy and boundless vision into a single concept: role models. It is not hard to believe that Dr. King would be pleased with some of today's role models and the opportunities presented to today's African American youth. And he would likely be displeased with others.

So in writing about black role models, we have tried to capture many of the experiences, perspectives, and thoughts of people who, like President Obama, are following in Dr. King's footsteps. Though they are not civil rights leaders or politicians, these men and women are trying to make a difference by making something of themselves professionally, modeling what it means to be successful, and reaching back to help others along the way.

In making something of themselves, they have advanced Dr. King's mission by becoming role models for future generations of African Americans, generations inspired by King and idolizing the Obamas. And they have done so while striving to make Dr. King's dream a reality not only for themselves, but also for youth, who can learn from their struggles and follow in their footsteps.

We honor them as real role models.

Acknowledgments

We must first extend a heartfelt thank-you to the twenty-three people who allowed us to share their stories in this book. Your stories are both awe inspiring and timeless.

Also, a number of people served as guiding lights and invaluable advisors for one or both of us during the making of this book. Their counsel, like that of all good role models, did not go unnoticed. The more we talked about this book with our friends and colleagues, the more we realized how blessed we are to have such wonderful people in our lives. The staff at the University of Texas Press, led by Theresa May, is certainly at the forefront of this group, along with Kip Keller, who did an amazing job of editing this work while maintaining its soul.

The movement Dr. King led was made up of ordinary people with an immeasurable ability to make a difference through collective energy and hard work. Each person who helped in the making of this book shares those same qualities.

The search for real role models in the African American community is ongoing. We thank each and every one of you for helping us push the search further along.

Introduction

Who is a real role model? Perhaps more important, what makes a real role model? This book helps answer those questions.

But before we examine those questions, I want to tell you a little bit about how this book came about, because I think doing so will help shed light on how Joah and I came to answer those questions. It started in early 2007, on what would have been Dr. King's seventy-eighth birthday. Needless to say, Dr. King has greatly influenced our lives, and this book is a testament to his continued legacy.

As a new member of the University of Texas at Austin's faculty, I was featured on the university's Web site in an article titled "Redefine the Finish Line." The article focused on my studies of how the "overemphasis on athletic success may limit academic pursuits for African-American children." I consider this one of my foremost areas of interest as both an educator and a father. The article posed two questions: "Why were African American kids given the message that they can become professional athletes when so few can? And how does this message limit the possibilities they pursue?" And then it quoted my general response to problem of pursuing sports success over any other dream: "I've always wanted to try to get people who thought they were going to be athletes to kind of back up and get a bigger perspective . . . because for most poor African Americans, it's not sport that's going to bring them out of poverty. It's education." The article concluded with these words:

He wants to see teachers give kids tools to use in their lives, and one of those tools is to understand there are many viable options for good careers outside of sports.

In getting that message across, Harrison may find he has help from his son . . . Today he teaches school in New Orleans.

God works in mysterious ways, and luckily he told Joah to read that article the day it was posted online. And it turns out Joah had written some words of his own that, coupled with the ideas I presented in that article, would become the foundation of this book. Here are a few of the words Joah shared with me that day:

These accomplished athletes, actors, comedians, talk-show hosts, and music moguls are far more likely to be considered role models by African-American youths than the African-American men and women who lead the companies they buy from, teach at the schools they send their children to or start the nonprofit organizations they donate thousands of dollars to. . . .

Dr. Martin Luther King, Jr. envisioned a nation without inequality in its effort to be a "land of opportunity." I envision a nation where we honor and embrace those overlooked contributors to Dr. King's mission.

It turned out that while Joah is younger than my son, he and I share many beliefs and life experiences. Both of us came from low-income mother-led homes where there didn't seem to be many options to making it out of our less-than-privileged circumstances unless we could do one of two things: put our heads down and score some touchdowns or put our heads down and score some As.

When we came together to start writing this book, we kept

coming back to what helped us "make it out" while many of our childhood friends and classmates stayed behind, their athletic or musical dreams deferred, as Langston Hughes once wrote. We quickly realized that the full answer was not simply a matter of what—education—but also of whom—role models.

Those people, those role models, we soon realized, weren't just ordinary people . . . well, not completely. They weren't just role models either; they were *real* role models. The people profiled in this book are also worthy of that designation.

Over the course of making this book, particularly through our interviews and discussions with the real role models themselves and other parents and professionals, we realized that being around these types of successful, well-rounded people is necessary for all young people, no matter what kind of home they grow up in, what kind of schools they attend, or what type of communities they are raised in.

From ages thirteen to twenty-one, many black youth, through no fault of their own, are forced to grow up much faster and experience many more challenges than their white counterparts. This reality has educational, familial, financial, and professional consequences. And though there is no single remedy for this problem, the combination of real role models and education can serve as a solid foundation.

The making of this book has strengthened our belief in that sentiment. In other words, although watching Michael Jordan play basketball on TV can't make you an NBA player, and watching Barack Obama give a speech can't make you a successful politician, they can inspire you to believe that you, too, can reach their level of accomplishment through hard work, focus, and self-discipline.

And who knows, maybe you can follow in the footsteps of Barack and Michelle Obama and become a real role model yourself.

LOUIS HARRISON, JR.

REAL ROLE MODELS

Part One

WHAT THEY ARE AND
WHY WE NEED THEM

CHAPTER 1

Why We Need Real Role Models

I am not a role model.

CHARLES BARKLEY, FORMER NBA MVP AND HALL OF FAMER

In the past fifteen years, much has been written—everything from then–first lady Hillary Clinton's "it takes a village to raise a child" to Barkley's famous words above—about the importance of parents, teachers, and mentors in helping children become successful adults. In this book we have not looked primarily at what mix of adult interaction is appropriate in order for young people to become formidable adults. Nor have we concerned ourselves with the question of whether athletes and entertainers should serve as role models, as Barkley would have us do. (In fact, many people in both professions prove themselves to be role models each day: Snoop Dogg sponsors a youth football league, Jay-Z raises awareness about the need for clean water in Africa, and Oprah Winfrey has inspired a generation of young black women.)

Instead, we focus on successful, and largely unknown, black professionals and what makes them real role models. We felt that it was important for the black community as a whole to consider what it means to be a real role model and which qualities of role models are worth emulating. We were especially interested in helping you—whether you are a high school student, a parent, or a teacher—get to know real role models who have gained little fame despite making a large difference in the lives of others.

And we aren't alone in seeing why real role models are so important. Trish Millines Dziko, the creator of AfricanAmerican RoleModels.com, wrote, "Nearly every time the discussion of African American role models comes up, the people who are mentioned are athletes, entertainers, hip hop and rap artists or they are dead. It is important for all children to see that African Americans are present, and hold leadership positions in, every profession. It is absolutely necessary that African American children see people who look like them being successful in something other than sports and entertainment."

It is no surprise that since many media outlets, from MTV to ESPN, glorify celebrities' lives, many young black people want to be the next Beyoncé or LeBron before they want to attend college or become a doctor or engineer. Put another way: while striving to achieve hoop dreams (or Hollywood dreams), many young blacks are having academic nightmares. Even Barkley himself, during an interview on CNN, said, "Most of our [black] role models are athletes and entertainers. We got to get black kids to be educated."

With those words, we come full circle. By sharing some amazing stories of people who used determination, hard work, and resilience to become successful, we hope to show you who should be considered a real role model. Today, even Charles Barkley agrees that real role models are necessary. And truth is, they can be found in many places besides basketball arenas, music studios, and movie sets. And the Oval Office is just one of the possibilities.

CHAPTER 2

Defining a Role Model

First, we must acknowledge there is no simple, single definition of the term *role model*. Sure, we can look to President Obama or First Lady Obama, but even then we would still not know exactly what a role model is.

We do, however, owe much of our common thinking on the term *role model* to Robert Merton, a longtime Columbia University professor and an award-winning sociologist, who died in 2003. Dr. Merton, in essence, believed that for young black students interested in a military career, retired four-star general and former secretary of state Colin Powell could serve as a role model; for aspiring basketball players, Michael Jordan; for aspiring filmmakers, Spike Lee; and so forth.

But today, profession should not limit a person's choice of role model. For example, although I (Spearman) never aspired to be a rapper, I have been inspired by Jay-Z for years and also by actor Will Smith. From these examples and the interviews conducted for this book, I have established a personal definition of a real role model: "A real role model is someone you admire who possesses and projects positive qualities that have helped him or her develop and grow, personally and professionally, and that inspire others to follow in his or her footsteps toward success."

This definition emphasizes positive qualities because real role models should double as good people. While it is unreasonable to think that being a real role model makes someone perfect (no one is), it is justifiable to expect a role model to be a good person, at least by our own standards. Also, the mention of personal and professional development indicates that a real role model understands the positive relationship between personal and professional success, and vice versa. Being a workaholic or wealthy person without any friends or family isn't the sign of a real role model. And the word *inspire* points to one of the main differences between simple role models and real role models: the acknowledgment of their influence on others. For an example of this, look at the interview with children's surgeon Dr. Tim George (Chapter 12), which shows that understanding your influence on a young person's life can make you more of a real role model than being a successful doctor.

This definition of a real role model goes only as far as this book takes it. As you read these pages, you should tweak it and form your own definition. Of course, some concepts and principles will be common to any definition of *role model;* we offer some guidance, but, in large part, it is up to you to find out about those within these stories.

Real role models can show you opportunities that are available both in your community and for your future. By following their example, you will be able to understand how one person's path to success can be used as a road map for your own—not so much to follow, but to help guide.

In many ways, that is exactly what real role models are—personal and professional road maps. Sure, they may not all be as rich and famous as Jay-Z or as accomplished and dignified as General Colin Powell, but they can all point the way to success and fulfillment for someone.

It is important that we do not expect real role models to be all things to all people or, especially, to be perfect. Instead, a real role model is someone who represents the kind of parent, person, or professional you admire and intend to be one day. No one's path will be identical to your own, but you can always learn from others who have traveled similar roads. So although there is no single image of a real role model, there are many ways to identify one. And it is up to you to be ready when a real role model steps into your life—or to become a real role model in someone else's life.

For example, in the 1994 movie *Above the Rim,* the main character has all the basketball skills he needs to make it to college, but he lacks the understanding required of a top-notch leader on the court or a responsible man off it. That is, until he meets a former basketball star who learned those tasks the hard way. Although initially reluctant, the younger player eventually realizes that the man is there to help him reach his potential by showing him how to avoid the pitfalls waiting to entrap him.

Sure, the movie didn't win any Academy Awards or make either of the main actors A-list stars, but that movie stands out from the thousands of others I have seen because it shows the making of a real role model. Like the lead character in that film, black teenagers and young adults must come to understand that there are people ready and willing to help them learn important lessons about life and thereby realize their full potential.

That is what Robert Merton and Dr. Martin Luther King, Jr., would want for each of us.

CHAPTER 3

They Are More Important than Ever

After this chapter, we will begin delving into the lives of some real role models. Here, we want to give you some hard facts about why we felt that talking about them, and not only in this book, is going to be increasingly important to the black community. It is important to understand that even if there were enough roster spots in the NBA for every aspiring point guard or enough openings on the *Billboard* charts each week for every hopeful singer, we would still need role models in hundreds of other careers and fields to ensure that all black students become professional somethings and that their careers will make them happy and make those around them better people. Simply put, we need more role models today than ever before. As some troubling trends and statistics show, the main institutions—family, church, school—black communities once relied on as sources of role models have rapidly declined and are being replaced by weaker, less sustainable or attainable sources of pride and empowerment, such as sports and entertainment.

During the civil rights movement, roughly the mid-1950s to the late 1960s, it was typical for black children to wake up in a two-parent home, attend schools staffed by young, eager black teachers, and to go to church each week. Today, too many black kids live in single-parent homes, are taught by teachers who lack the cultural competence to effectively teach them, rarely attend church, and are frequently found watching television or playing video games. The makeup of the black home and community is changing dramatically, and young black people are paying a steep price.

Frank Harold Wilson, a sociology professor at the University of Wisconsin–Milwaukee, echoed this sentiment when he said that the "church, school and community that reinforced the [black] family are increasingly challenged by new social controls of the media, peer groups and 'the street.'"

Before the civil rights movement, the foundations in the black community consisted generally of a family led by both parents, an education system that spent more time teaching than testing, and a church that made religion a major part of a young black person's upbringing. Since the civil rights movement, each of these sources of identity and information has steeply declined, beginning with the family. In 2003, *Ebony* magazine's Joy Bennett Kinnon wrote, "The shocking state of Black marriage: experts say many will never get married." She went on to provide some historical perspective:

In 1963 when Dr. Martin Luther King, Jr. gave his "I Have a Dream" speech, more than 70 percent of all Black families were headed by married couples. In 2002 that number was 48 percent. . . .

Thus, we have another major crisis on our hands. Quiet as it's kept, we are confronted with one of the biggest crises in the history of African-American people.

Research indicates black family structure has weakened more in the few decades since the end of the civil rights movement than in the century that preceded it. There are a number of reasons for this, several of which also effect nonblacks. University of Virginia professor W. Bradford Wilcox conducted a study titled "Religion, Race, and Relationships in Urban America," and the findings have harsh implications for our community: "As a consequence of the retreat from marriage, African American, Latino, and poor children in urban America are much more likely to spend time in a single-parent family or a fragile family compared to White middle-class American children." Also, two University of California–Davis professors, Marianne Page and Ann Huff Stevens, discovered that "divorce and marriage play much bigger economic roles for black children than white children in the United States." Their research found that "in the first two years following a divorce, family income among white children falls about 30 percent, while it falls by 53 percent among black children."

Declining rates of marriage and the resulting economic disadvantages only somewhat explain why so many young black men and women end up on the streets instead of college campuses. They also help explain why so many young black adults, like the ones who buy fancy clothes and cars rather than saving money or buying homes, look at millionaire celebrities as role models; it is easier to envision a better life for yourself—with the kind of financial comfort and security that celebrities have—by working for things that seem within reach, like cars and clothes.

But the surest way for our youth to obtain those material things is to build on their educational foundation. Unfortunately, some statistics indicate black students face far tougher hurdles to academic success than their counterparts. For example, a U.S. Department of Education study showed that while 38 percent of white students believed it was important for them to help people in the community, 54 percent of African American students said the same. Similarly, only 15 percent of white students said it was important to correct social and economic inequalities, while more than 30 percent of blacks said so. Black students, it seems, understand the disparities between their worlds and those of their white counterparts. Watching an NBA game or a music video full of happy black faces may seem like a reasonable way to escape this reality.

While roughly the same percentage of black and white students are enrolled in school, when compared to their white peers, proportionally a quarter more black students go to schools with security guards, six times as many walk through metal detectors to enter school, and five times as many have bars on their classroom windows. Such grim conditions may explain why so many black students have difficulty identifying school as a positive place where hard work and commitment can make dreams come true. Too often, black students embrace after-school basketball or football practice more than the subjects they study during the day.

However, there are signs of educational improvement in the black community. The last fifteen years have seen increases in the proportion of our children who are read to before kindergarten (up 10 percentage points), and who are taught words and numbers before they begin school (up 15 points).

But even as more black students appear prepared to enter school and more black students make it all the way to college, fewer black college graduates are becoming teachers. The number of black college graduates who choose to teach middle school or high school has declined in recent decades as many seek more lucrative jobs in business, communications, and law. In a 2000 *Black Collegian* article titled "The Role of the African-American Teacher: Why It's Essential in the School System," Gilbert Brown reported insights from teachers and education researchers. They were all concerned with the declining number of black teachers.

Brown quoted Dr. Kate Conway-Turner, chair of the Department of Individual and Family Studies at the University of Delaware:

During the elementary and secondary years, a child is going through the process of shaping the person he or she will be. . . . All the foundation is laid there—not just the academic foundation, but the child's sense of self. That's why it's so important for kids to see models of people like themselves in the school system. It's very difficult, but not impossible, when you're trying to figure out who you are and the kinds of things that you aspire to do when you don't see reflections of yourself.

Although the number of black teachers is dwindling, our youth can still go to one place where they can see people who look like them and present positive images: the church. From the time of slavery, when black men and women sang hymns in cotton fields, through the civil rights movement, when Dr. King and others were pastors before they were national leaders, religion has been central to the black community. Even the militant Nation of Islam, with Malcolm X at the podium, had its roots in the Muslim faith, and James Brown's secular pop songs had their roots in gospel music.

An article on Professor Wilcox's study, mentioned above, summarized several key findings: attending church helps bolster marriage rates, improve relationships, and enhance fatherhood within the black community.

Religious initiatives that seek to increase paternal church attendance will serve the welfare of countless children and communities who depend upon strong and healthy families to survive and thrive. . . .

Marriage provides an array of economic and social benefits to children, adults and the communities in which they live, and these benefits extend to poor and minority communities in urban America.

While church remains strong within the black community, there are reasons to believe the number of role models produced by churches is declining. For example, in previous decades, black children were expected to go to church with their parents, but as two-parent homes become single-parent homes, the frequency of churchgoing has seemingly declined.

Likewise, Dr. King's and Malcolm X's voices have never been filled to the same uplifting degree by their oftentimes self-appointed successors.

Even gospel music has suffered from the decline in church-going, as Kirk Franklin and others have tried to use R&B and rap-music elements to draw young people back to church. This is a great departure from past decades, when musical inspiration ran the opposite way and R&B and blues artists such as Ray Charles and Mariah Carey gained fame for sounding like gospel singers.

Also, while Dr. King and other local pastors were heralded within the community, modern pastors are often treated with greater skepticism. One black pastor in Indiana drove to church in a Rolls-Royce purchased with the congregation's tithes, and televised pastors have made millions more than Dr. King ever did. While we recognize that most churches and pastors do not operate this way, how are we to be certain that black churches are producing real role models? How far away is the day when our religious leaders become no different from NFL wide receiver Terrell Owens and former NBA all-star Latrell Sprewell, who claimed they could not play for six or seven million dollars a year, because it was below their market value.

But this money-driven society is the one we now live in. Marriage is broken, the education system is failing, and church Sunday has become Super Bowl Sunday. Nowadays, black youths may be as likely to attend football practice as Bible study and may spend more time listening to Beyoncé or Kanye West than concentrating on earning As and Bs. Even listening to the "I Have a Dream" speech on the radio or to gospel music on the stereo has been replaced by watching an MLK tribute on BET's *106 & Park* after the latest hit song.

These transitions have infiltrated all aspects of black community and culture. In the first half of the last century, black children were encouraged to help their parents around the house. Today, black children are often encouraged to get jobs—not to help out their parents, but to buy a PlayStation or diamond-studded earrings.

The institutions of yesteryear are being replaced by the trends of tomorrow—where information comes from many more places than the family, the school, and the church. Now more than ever in the black community, it is important to recognize real role models.

Lynn Tyson

Willie Miles, Jr.

Horace Allen

Deavra Daughtry

Victoria Holloway Barbosa

Leonard Pitts, Jr.

Ed Stewart

Eric Motley

Tracie Hall

Kimberlydawn Wisdom

Steve Jones   Gloria Ladson-Billings

Bernard Muir

Craig Littlepage   Beverly Kearney

Part Two

WHO THEY ARE

CHAPTER 4

Moms

OUR PERSONAL REAL ROLE MODELS

Charles Barkley may have had something right about role models: parents sometimes make the best ones. In fact, it isn't uncommon for people to consider their parents a personal source of inspiration. A 2007 AP-MTV poll found that parents are chosen as heroes more often than any celebrity or friend or teacher: 29 percent of the teens and young adults named their mothers as heroes, 21 percent named their fathers, and 16 percent listed their parents without specifying one or the other.

This appears to be the standard for young blacks especially. Every week, it seems, we hear a rapper or singer, an actor or athlete, or even a college or high school graduate thank mom or dad for their helping on the road to success. Expressions of gratitude include Tupac's song "Dear Mama," Kanye West's "Hey Mama," NBA all-star Michael Redd building his pastor-father a church, and Tiger Woods crediting his father for his passion and success in golf.

Some say the symbolic nature of black parents as role models can be traced to African tribes, in which parents and eldest family members were treated with high esteem by their children. Others credit the strong role of mothers in the black community to the frequency of fatherless homes and to the tendency of children to form a strong attachment to a lone, positive parental figure. Both are probably right.

In light of this, we felt it necessary to talk a little more about our inspiration for putting this book together. No matter how many articles and books we read, how many successful black professionals we met, or how many words we wrote, the two of us approached this book with our own perspectives and ideas about what it means to be a real role model. It turned out we weren't all that far apart.

These next few words are about our real role models. Our mothers, Emily Sylva and Sabrena Spearman.

LOUIS HARRISON, JR.

My mother is the prototype of the strong black matriarch. The main attributes I received from her were perseverance and consistency. As with many of the important lessons of life, perseverance wasn't taught through verbal instructions, it was demonstrated day in and day out.

Now, as a parent myself, I look back and wonder how my mother reared four sons on a school cafeteria worker's salary while keeping us out of the criminal justice system. Her formula was a simple one. She went to work everyday, worked hard, and demanded the same from her sons.

When we failed to meet her demands, she was consistent in holding us accountable and providing stern consequences for any offenses. Let me put it plainly. She gave us all responsibilities and whipped our butts if we didn't do what she told us to do. If I didn't understand her parenting fully as a youth, I definitely do now.

This remarkable woman, who never finished high school, became the proud parent of a naval captain, a university professor, a quality-inspection engineer, and a photographer. Though she did not have the opportunity to get an education herself, she encouraged, expected, and pushed us to do so.

Though she was tough at times, my mother had a soft heart.

She was the neighborhood cook and baker. She would always share whatever she had with whoever needed it. Many of the neighborhood children knew that if they hung out with us, they would have a meal and a piece of cake or some cookies. My mother would not even think of sending our friends home without offering them something to eat. To this day, my mother's most satisfying activities are cooking, baking, and watching others enjoy the fruit of her labor. Only recently, because of overwhelming demand, has she began charging people for her cakes.

As the oldest of the four children, I shouldered much of the responsibility for my brothers. Though I abused my authority in many instances (and paid dearly when she found out), the notion of being responsible and fulfilling my duties was deeply ingrained in me. One of the complaints we hear today about our youth is the irresponsibility they demonstrate. This wasn't an option with my mother.

Whether it was washing dishes (which I learned to do before I was tall enough to reach the sink) or washing and folding clothes, she held us responsible for completing our chores and demanded a high standard of quality in everything we did.

I must also give credit to my father's memory. Though, like all of us, he had his share of shortcomings, he maintained a relationship with us until his death. Before he and my mother divorced, he was the disciplinarian, sternly keeping my brothers and me in line.

I had many members of my large family who served as role models in different areas of life. My father and many of my uncles were very handy in both construction and mechanics. Just hanging around them I learned to perform many tasks that most would have to call repairmen to do. Very seldom do I recall my father or uncles taking their cars to a repair shop or calling a plumber, electrician, or anyone to fix problems around the house. They always took care of things themselves.

I inherited that trait, although I don't hesitate to call for help when I need it, because, as you know, I am a professor, not a handyman, by trade.

I had other family role models. I had an uncle who taught me to manage money, another taught me to fish, while others were patient enough to teach me a few carpentry skills. To all of them, I extend my deepest appreciation.

Others in my family provided a listening ear for my problems and gave me sound advice and encouragement. To them, I owe a debt of gratitude. I hesitate to call names, for there were so many contributors that I would surely leave someone out. But to all of my family, whether by blood or authentic friendship, I truly thank you all for what you have given to my life.

More recently, as I have acknowledged my call to ministry, God has graciously provided several role models in the teaching and preaching of his word. To them also I give thanks for the leadership provided, the encouragement given, and their endurance of my boring attempts at proclaiming God's word. I thank God for placing so many excellent role models in my life.

While none of these role models demonstrate perfection, I do have a role model that is perfect. The more I study the life of Jesus Christ, the more I believe he has been my perfect role model. The life of Christ and the lessons he teaches provide the perfect model for life. None of us can live up to that standard, so Joah and I have tried to provide examples of people who in one way or another provide models of excellence. In this regard, they are similar to my mother. They, too, are real role models.

JOAH SPEARMAN

I have always believed God places certain people in your life at certain times. I have been blessed with a great number of influential people throughout my life: high school friends who let me be myself, and mentors who have helped me make the most of myself. Throughout, there has been one person who has always been in my life. That person has been my mother. Without insufficiently stating her impact and influence on the person I am and aspire to become, I must say my mother is the only real role model I have ever had.

Oftentimes, children in disadvantaged or low-income environments lack true role models. Instead, they wind up idolizing professional athletes, entertainers, and musicians. And these individuals often make contributions to their communities, particularly black and inner-city communities. But I was blessed with a truly one-of-a-kind role model in my own home and my life each and everyday.

My mother was always there to make sure her three boys would grow to become three successful men. As the youngest of that trio, I am proud to let her know I wholeheartedly believe she couldn't have done a better job. She isn't the only single mother to rear three children (boys especially). Nor is she the only woman to raise herself and her family out of welfare. However, my mother is the only mother I have ever had, and she has doubled as the most dedicated and hardworking person I have ever known.

Now I bring this up not to profile my mother, the obstacles she faced and overcame, and the feats she accomplished, but more to share the many lessons she taught me. Among them are prioritizing, patience, and planning. These three Ps are the most important lessons my mother shared with me.

Prioritizing refers to the ability to set goals and follow through with them. The significance of this life lesson cannot be overstated. While my father was halfway across the country doing God knows what, my mother made sure my brothers and I were being provided for. She went on the occasional date, had fun, and made sure to spend time with friends, but mostly, my mom was working overtime, putting a meal on the dinner table, or shopping for bargains at the local Goodwill or K-Mart.

From this, I learned that only through efficient and careful prioritizing can one achieve anything worth being proud of. Thanks in large part to my mother's encouragement, I was able to make education a top priority in my life from a very young age. Though no one in my family had a college degree, I always knew I would graduate from a prestigious public university where I could learn from the best and learn with the brightest. It was my priority.

As a seventh grader, I jotted down the University of Texas at Austin as a possible college choice. Ten years later, I walked across the stage as a graduate of that same school with a degree in hand. My mother was watching, eyes watering and gleaming all at once.

Today, I continue setting goals and prioritizing in order to achieve them, but achieving anything requires a great deal of patience. Thankfully, again, I learned from the best.

For nearly twenty-five years, my mother strived to purchase her own home. She went from minimum wage to her current salary—which is still less than I was making just one year out of college—with that same goal in mind. As many single mothers can attest, she spent many of those years repairing the credit mishaps of younger years and enduring pay raises of fifty cents or a dollar at a time. Still, many more of those years were spent simply being patient.

Finally, at the youthful age of forty-five, my mother accomplished her greatest feat: she became a homeowner. For some, owning a home is not a noteworthy accomplishment, either because they grew up in a home their entire lives or because their careers enabled them to own theirs as young adults. But for my mother, this was a crowning achievement.

Following in the footsteps of my mother, I have learned the importance of patience. Not even a full year into my postcollege experience in Washington, D.C., I contemplated moving back to Austin, where I was already comfortable. But remembering my mother's lesson of patience at just the right moment, I remained in our nation's capital. The funny thing is, Louis lives in Austin and teaches at my alma mater, but I probably would never have met him had I moved back to Austin. Good things come to those who are patient, not those who wait.

Will I be rewarded for my patience? So far, all signs point to yes. However, even with all the prioritizing and patience in the world, I wouldn't be anywhere without the detailed planning I have put into most everything I have gotten myself into. That too, is a lesson learned from my mother.

More times than I care to remember, I have seen capable members of the black community—my family included—fail to reach their dreams, whether they involved buying a new car or getting a new job, because of poor planning. The necessary ambition, drive, and talent may have all been there, but the planning was always a second (or third) thought. Whereas Tiger Woods had his father, Earl, who planned a course enabling his son to master golf skills and reach lofty goals, many other young black men grow up without fathers to show them the benefits of a good plan. And many young black women lack the know-how to avoid the social ills that force them into all-too-familiar positions as teen or young mothers instead of college students, girls around the way instead of women on their way.

I, too, missed many of the lessons and comforts that growing up with a father would have provided, but my mother never let me miss out on the lesson of good planning. Whether deciding how to spend my summer-job money or my after-school time, I did my best to keep my mother's planning practices in mind. I realize that the same planning skills that helped her reach her home-owning goal have and will continue to help me reach my life's goals.

Set priorities, be patient, and make a plan: my mother

never said those words precisely, but she put them into practice every single day. As I grow older and set loftier goals, the examples and lessons she provided continue to serve as my life's compass.

Creating a path to success, providing life lessons for avoiding or overcoming obstacles, and leading by example are the true qualities of my real role model. We may not all have both mothers and fathers. Some of us may even go without either, instead relying on grandparents, guardians, and others. Still, as I mentioned earlier, God finds a way to put someone in your life who may be able to fill this critical role.

I am sure a great many of you, like myself, owe much to your role models. And you can repay them only by meeting your potential. I hope my mother is happy knowing that I have reached where I am today by keeping the lessons she taught me close to heart.

The following chapters show that, like our mothers, sometimes the best role models are people you would never see on TV. They may be public servants striving to make a difference, reporters covering a story that is important to the black community, or artists sharing their creativity for the greater good.

CHAPTER 5

Rufus Cormier, JD

PARTNER AT THE BAKER BOTTS LAW FIRM

Rufus Cormier's journey began in Beaumont, an oil-refinery town an hour north of Houston, where he would later make his mark. Cormier grew up as the son of a Baptist minister father and a mother who owned a local grocery store owner. In the sixties, Beaumont had not fully embraced the civil rights movement, and Cormier was taught by black teachers in segregated schools.

The journey from Beaumont to Houston led to three decades of success for the award-winning lawyer. Today he is one of the most respected attorneys, black or white, in one of the nation's savviest cities for politics or business. For each of the last five years he has been recognized by *Texas Monthly* magazine and *Law & Politics* as a "Texas Super Lawyer."

For Cormier, a large part of his success in moving from an oil town to downtown is attributable to succeeding in the classroom. Having grown up with a father who loved outdoor work—raising chickens, landscaping, and gardening—Cormier realized early on that his schoolwork could help him avoid such work and at the same time earn praise from his teachers. "Education has been the most dominant force in my life. I learned early on that there were numerous perks associated with doing well in school and that the difference between the effort required to perform satisfactorily and that required to do very well was not that great. I recognized around third grade that tremendous benefits could be derived from doing well in school," recounted Cormier.

Despite his academic success, Cormier was unsure of where to channel his energy. He remembered, "I thought about [what I wanted to do] a great deal. However, I was somewhat unfocused. The only professional blacks I knew were educators, who I greatly admired. There were a couple of black doctors and lawyers in Beaumont, but I did not know them personally. I wasn't certain as a youngster of the direction I wanted to take."

In high school, he found football. His idol was the legendary running back Jim Brown, and Cormier too was pretty good at the sport. He earned a scholarship to play for Southern Methodist University as a member of the second class of African American athletes allowed to play football in the Southwest Conference. At SMU, he was co-captain of the football team, named outstanding defensive player in the 1968 Bluebonnet Bowl, and named to the second consensus All–Southwest Conference team. He thought, at the time, that he would play professionally and, only after retiring from the sport, pursue a professional career. "I really loved academic pursuits as well as athletics. While I aspired to be a professional athlete, I knew that was a short-term proposition even if I was fortunate enough to achieve that goal at all. Consequently, I focused on preparing for the long term. Not only did I recognize that education was important, I enjoyed academic activity. I really loved school," Cormier added.

It wasn't until Cormier's senior year of college that he considered a career in law. In fact, it was through a conversation with the husband of one of his high school teachers, an attorney in Beaumont, that he was introduced to the idea of attending law school. As an anthropology major, Cormier had considered pursuing a doctorate in anthropology and becoming a college professor, with an eye toward eventual involvement in politics. After speaking with law professors at SMU and talking more with the Beaumont attorney, he became convinced that the practice of law would be a better route into politics.

After receiving the Avella Winn Hay Achievement Award from SMU as its outstanding senior student, Cormier headed for Yale, home to one of the nation's premier law schools. Three years later, law degree in hand, Cormier landed a position coveted by thousands of students—a staff job on the House Judiciary Committee as a special assistant during the impeachment proceedings against then-president Richard Nixon.

Shortly thereafter, Cormier moved to Houston to join the Baker Botts law firm. Seven years later, he became the first African American to be named partner at a major Houston law firm. Cormier's practice encompasses commercial banking, finance, and general corporate matters for leading financial institutions and technology, manufacturing, and service-oriented businesses.

Cormier's story makes getting from a Beaumont backyard to a Houston boardroom look simple, but he credited his success to his education and his dedication to professional excellence: "I believe that it is self evident that education is the most effective means of escaping economic deprivation and its accompanying social ills. The advice that I would give any young person is that the rewards of education are so great that there is no rational reason not to take advantage of available educational opportunities."

Cormier stressed the need for diligence and tenacity: "Some young people seem to think that there are constraints on their ability to achieve, but the fact is that there are tremendous opportunities for success if one is willing to take advantage of them. I was confident that I would succeed if I worked to achieve my goals, and that confidence inspired me to exert the effort required—regardless of the obstacles that I encountered. I think that if I were to quote anyone on the requirements for success, it would be [former secretary of state] Colin Powell, who, when asked by a young person about the secrets of success, answered, 'There are no secrets of success; one succeeds by setting goals and being willing to work as hard as necessary to achieve them.'"

Rufus Cormier didn't set the goal of becoming a successful lawyer until he was twenty-one years old, but he has certainly achieved what he set out to do. And to think that he found that success only an hour away from his hometown.

Melody Barnes

DIRECTOR OF THE WHITE HOUSE DOMESTIC
POLICY COUNCIL

Just as Kobe Bryant and LeBron James benefited from watching Michael Jordan and Magic Johnson play, real role models today have benefited from the paths charted by their predecessors. Ella Baker, a Virginia-born woman and critical voice during the civil rights movement, blazed a path for millions of blacks, particularly women, to follow. Melody Barnes is one of the women trying to follow in her footsteps.

Baker and Barnes have a number of similarities. Both were originally from Virginia, both moved to North Carolina—Baker during her childhood, Barnes during college—and both committed themselves to improving the lives of others.

While Baker grew up in a time when teaching was one of the few professional jobs open to black women, Barnes has grown up in a time when black people have typically pursued better-paying professions.

After working as a key staffer for the NAACP for fifteen years, Baker took her organizational skills to the Southern Christian Leadership Conference (SCLC), an organization cofounded by Dr. King, where she became a respected and trusted advisor and helped lead voter-registration initiatives. Eventually, she became the SCLC's leader in Atlanta, where she made her greatest impact by inviting students to join the civil rights movement. This resulted in the creation of the Student Nonviolent Coordinating Committee, or SNCC (pronounced "snick").

As SNCC became took on a major role in the movement, Baker spread her influence to social-justice issues, working with the Southern Conference Education Fund to help change political party rules to allow blacks to serve as delegates to the national conventions. This was the first time that blacks had played a major part in the presidential political process. Time and time again, Baker made her presence felt wherever she lent her support.

For this and for her leadership and persistence, Melody Barnes credits Baker as her real role model. "I was very interested in history and the civil rights movement growing up. Ella Baker was amazing to me because she helped make the woman's role in this church-based movement," said Barnes. "Her recognition of youth and the role students could play in the movement was cutting edge even in a cutting-edge movement."

Involving students in the civil rights movement was truly progressive. Students, after all, ended up becoming some of the loudest voices in the movement and some of the most outspoken critics of the Vietnam War throughout the sixties and the early seventies. Fittingly, Barnes mirrors Baker in yet another way: she has worked to usher that progressive era back in, in hopes of reversing domestic and foreign policies that have, among other things, helped put the United States in the middle of another fairly unpopular war. "We have to rebuild the progressive infrastructure in order to make change on a big scale," said Barnes. "Hopefully, we can help move the nation to a better place."

Like Baker in her day, Barnes says "we" when speaking about her cause. Only in Barnes's case, she is not referring to the NAACP and the civil rights movement. Barnes's "we" has stood for all U.S. taxpayers and the voting public since she joined the White House staff to serve as director of President Obama's Domestic Policy Council.

Barnes joined Obama's campaign staff after working as executive vice president for policy at the Center for American Progress, a Washington, D.C.–area think tank that has become a leading policy organization. As senior policy advisor to then-senator Obama, Barnes helped craft his stances on education and health care, two areas of great importance to voters. Now Barnes is charged with helping the president lead the country into the future, focusing on improving schools, hospitals, and other public services that all Americans depend on, especially during the ongoing economic crises facing the country.

Like her boss, Barnes has a tough and challenging job ahead of her, but like Ella Baker, she is up to the task.

"I was always interested in government and history," said Barnes. "I volunteered on campaigns, and I grew up in a community where parents engaged their kids. My parents were active in the community, so there was always a sense of volunteerism and public service." That sense of volunteerism and public service came from her mother, a schoolteacher, and her father, a civilian employee for the U.S. Army.

During her youth, Barnes was inspired by educators as well as her parents. She credits both a black high school teacher and a college professor with being her first nonparental role models and mentors. "There are different kinds of role models," said Barnes. "They have the most influence when it's people you know and you can watch how they walk through their day and they help give you a sense of something to strive for."

Upon graduating from the University of North Carolina with a history degree, Barnes went on to law school at the University of Michigan, believing that a legal education would equip her with the broad and in-depth knowledge to make a big impact in government. "I wanted a way to serve, and the role law plays in government and [the] civil rights movement and the Constitution interested me," said Barnes. "I wanted to effect big change and help people."

After gaining experience as an attorney in New York for a few years following law school, Barnes moved to Washington, D.C., where she began doing her part to help others. As assistant counsel to the U.S. House of Representatives Judiciary Subcommittee on Civil and Constitutional Rights, Barnes worked in Congress to pass the Voting Rights Improvement Act of 1992, which built upon the 1965 law passed during Baker's and Dr. King's era.

Based on her record of working on diversity and judicial issues in Congress, Barnes was appointed director of legislative affairs for the Equal Employment Opportunity Commission under then-president Bill Clinton, certainly one of the more progressive presidents on matters of diversity. Soon thereafter, she became the chief lawyer for Senator Edward "Ted" Kennedy on the Senate Judiciary Committee.

Working for Kennedy gave Barnes a chance to learn from one of the longest-tenured and most well-respected members of Congress. Barnes did everything from help shape legislation on civil rights and women's rights, to helping a woman and her child obtain legal help to get away from an abusive husband. After eight years in that role, Barnes joined the Center for American Progress.

Along with her professional experiences and ties, Barnes is on the board of directors of EMILY's List, one of the most powerful political groups in the country for women seeking public office, and the Constitution Project, which "seeks consensus solutions to difficult legal and constitutional issues." She is also a board member of the Maya Angelou Public Charter School in Washington, D.C.

Through her many professional and personal endeavors, Barnes has demonstrated her commitment to making a positive difference in the world.

"Who you are and what makes you tick gives your life meaning. I think everyone can live life with an ethic of public service, whether that's volunteering, conservation, or community service," said Barnes. "Anyone can shape and touch other people, not just rappers, actors, and celebrities. There are always people trying to make your life better."

Those people Barnes refers to are the ones she considers the real role models. She admits that she once judged potential role models solely on their professional accomplishments, but that has since changed. Perhaps it is because she herself is now one of the people she describes. "Before, I looked at accomplishments, and I was more ends oriented, and I looked at society's measure of success," said Barnes. "Now, I admire their journey and look at the person they appear to be. Everyone can have relevance and [be a role model], regardless of if you're a singer, scientist, or stay-at-home parent."

Like Baker, Barnes realized that even while working behind the scenes, she had to set a visible example for young blacks: "It's unrealistic to think kids aren't looking beyond their own [parents]."

We will never know what Ella Baker's definition of a role model was, but we know that both she and Melody Barnes fit the following description. "A role model's entire life is directed toward something meaningful. It's a combination of personal and professional success that reflect one another," said Barnes. "I learned the most from people who desired a life of meaning and had a standard of excellence in everything they did."

As is often the case, a civil rights leader blazed a path that one of today's black leaders is doing an excellent job of following.

CHAPTER 7

Eric Motley, PhD

MANAGING DIRECTOR OF THE ASPEN INSTITUTE'S HENRY CROWN FELLOWSHIP PROGRAM

Madeline Albright, an appointee of President Bill Clinton, was the first female secretary of state in U.S. history. One of Clinton's predecessors, Lyndon Johnson, had a good friend named Jack Valenti, who left the White House to become Hollywood's top voice in Washington, D.C., for nearly four decades as head of the Motion Picture Association of America (MPAA). What do Albright and Valenti have in common? Both were major players in Washington with a connection to the Aspen Institute, an organization committed to "timeless values, enlightened leadership."

The Aspen Institute is now home to Eric Motley, who might follow in their footsteps and become a Washington insider, regardless of whether politics have anything to do with it.

Motley, thirty-four, is a native of Montgomery, Alabama. He has never met his father, and his mother gave him up at birth. Thankfully, his mother's adoptive parents took him up, and he never lacked for parental guidance. And politics may have always been in his future, since his late grandfather's name was George Washington.

G. W. Motley, however, wasn't a famous general or politician, instead working as a jack-of-all-trades and expert carpenter who helped build churches in Montgomery, including Union Chapel AME Zion Church, which his family attended. Most of young Eric Motley's values, both political and personal, seemed to stem from his grandfather.

Speaking of roots, Motley attributes much of his character and success to growing up in a rural southern community still dotted with cotton fields and plantation homes. Away from city lights and the distractions prone to affect the upbringing of low-income minorities, he was able to learn about patience and timing. Motley has said he benefited from "growing up in that type of community where you have to learn about the processes of time."

Motley was a bit of an individualist during his Alabama youth. Realizing this, his grandfather taught Motley about authenticity and being comfortable in his own skin. Unlike children who sought to fit in and follow the crowd through the right mix of comedy, clothing, and compromises, Motley satisfied his innate sense of curiosity by reading books and becoming well versed in great literature, including the poetic works of Alfred, Lord Tennyson.

It comes as no coincidence that a line from one of Tennyson's greatest works, "Ulysses," inspired Motley tremendously: "To follow knowledge like a sinking star." Those words echo the important role education has played in Motley's life, dating back to his early childhood. He recalls peppering with questions—"What's that there?" and "Why are you doing that?"—a doctor who was treating his grandfather.

Motley became a regular winner on the high-school speaker circuit before heading to Samford University, in Birmingham, where he continued improving his prospects. Motley began exploring his political interests as an undergraduate, becoming involved in the Young Republicans and running the school's speakers series. He brought in such famous folks as poet Gwendolyn Brooks, presidential candidates Michael Dukakis and Ralph Nader, and Supreme Court Justice Clarence Thomas.

A few years earlier, Motley had written a letter of support to Justice Thomas during his tough confirmation process; later the lone black member of the nation's highest court shook his hand before giving an on-campus speech.

Another seminal influence in Motley's political makeup may

have been the occasions when, as a high school student, he saw the elderly George Wallace, the former Alabama governor who once stood up for segregation in public schools, opposing Dr. King and the civil rights movement. Motley looked at the man who had served as a symbol of the nation's racially divided past and saw himself as a potential symbol of America's racially blind future, where education and hard work, not skin color, would determine one's path.

After graduating from Samford in 1996, Motley—with encouragement from professors and financial support from an area businessman—set off for Scotland to continue his education. Upon arrival at St. Andrews University, Motley pursued a liberal arts master's degree, then remained at the school as a John Steven Watson Scholar while completing a PhD in international relations.

Two years after his return to the states, Motley became a special assistant to President George W. Bush. At twenty-nine, he was overseeing part of the president's personnel office, managing the appointment process for more than 1,200 positions. Motley, always able to pull people together, was charged with recommending individuals from around the country for key boards and presidential commissions, including those of the Kennedy Center and the Library of Congress; he himself served on the IRS Oversight Board and the National Institute of Health's National Cancer Institute Panel.

In the service of the president, Motley met hundreds of influential people from around the world, and some have voiced support for his return to Alabama should he desire a run for public office.

Henry Crown made his fortune building one of the nation's leading defense contractors, General Dynamics. But he made his biggest impact by becoming a major philanthropist, first in Chicago and then across the country. One of the beneficiaries

of Crown's philanthropy was the Aspen Institute, a nonprofit
organization devoted to improving leadership and encouraging
the discussion of contemporary problems. Now Motley is ex-
tending Crown's legacy, and making his own impact in the process, as managing director of the institute's Henry Crown Fel-
lowship Program. The organization's website says the program
seeks to train the "next generation of community-spirited
leaders, providing them with the tools necessary to meet the
challenges of corporate and civic leadership in the 21st century." Both Colin Powell's son Michael, who was head of the
Federal Communications Commission, and Motley are among
the dozens of other past and present senior government officials and Fortune 500 executives who have gone through the
program.

Before joining Aspen, Motley was already fostering leadership as director of the Office of International Visitors at the
State Department, the position he moved to after his stint in
the president's personnel office. In this capacity, Motley led
a staff of more than 100 and oversaw a budget of around $80
million while working closely under Bush confidant and longtime advisor Karen Hughes, then under secretary for public
diplomacy. Motley worked with embassies abroad to identify
emerging leaders through the International Visitor Leadership
Program, which brings roughly 5,000 foreign nationals from
around the globe to form connections and learn the American
way of doing politics. One such example was a group of HIV-
infected mothers from South Africa who came to learn about
AIDS prevention in America.

At Aspen, Motley is making his presence felt and making
strides toward lasting impact. Maybe he will follow in the footsteps of Secretaries of State Albright, Powell, or Rice.

Motley has frequently given a speech titled "An Odyssey of
Gratitude and Grace." Wherever he gives it—at universities,
conferences, or public events—he shares lessons from his upbringing and career while recounting the grace of others who

have helped him reach his current position, from George W. Motley to George W. Bush. Many of these instances of grace were chronicled in a *Washington Post* article in June 2006. Motley was portrayed as an odd but fast-rising black man in the Republican Party, as having fought a battle for his "political soul," since it is uncommon for a black man from the Deep South to be a Republican.

However, Motley disagrees with the notion that his soul was ever a prize to be fought over. Instead, he was taught from a young age to be comfortable thinking independently, being himself, and embracing the atypical. Fittingly, the *Post* article was titled "A Path All His Own." Eric Motley believes his path is one you shouldn't be afraid to follow.

CHAPTER 8

James McIntyre

SPOKESMAN FOR THE FEDERAL EMERGENCY
MANAGEMENT AGENCY

Public service has been a critical part of black history in America from the day Crispus Attucks became the first man to die in the Revolutionary War to the day General Colin Powell became the first black person to serve as U.S. secretary of state.

You may not know his name, but James McIntyre is another dedicated black public servant. During a period when government officials routinely made the news because of corruption and scandal, McIntyre worked behind the scenes to help people during a very tough time.

As a senior public affairs officer for the Federal Emergency Management Agency (FEMA), and lifetime government employee, McIntyre remained unscathed by the politically driven and ill-advised decision making that occurred in the aftermath of Hurricane Katrina. Instead, McIntyre and his senior colleagues helped disseminate critical information from a field office in Louisiana to victims of the devastating storm. It may be hard to imagine that conditions in New Orleans could have been worse, but without the efforts of McIntyre and other key officials who were not caught up in the political chaos surrounding the disaster, the state of affairs would have been dire in the extreme.

In New Orleans, McIntyre was able to draw on his experience in assisting after another national tragedy. After the planes hit the World Trade Center and the Pentagon, and another crashed in Pennsylvania on its way to Washington, D.C., on September 11, 2001, he helped set up the news desk for FEMA, which answered thousands of calls from the media and concerned citizens.

Even before 9/11 and Katrina, McIntyre was familiar with disasters. His first assignment with FEMA was to help victims of tornadoes that struck Oklahoma in 1998. Before that, he had a career in the U.S. Air Force, having been drafted in 1971 in the midst of the Vietnam War. "I was in the air force for twenty-four years and had a great career, and they gave me a lot of opportunities," said McIntyre. "But when I saw the devastation from that tornado and the resiliency those people had to get back, I thought, 'This is where I belong.'"

When he was drafted, McIntyre was studying political science at Tennessee State University, in Nashville, in hopes of someday becoming a lawyer. To stay close to that field, he worked in law enforcement as a military policeman for the air force. Over the next twenty-four years, McIntyre was stationed all over the country (in Alabama, Michigan, Washington, Texas, North Dakota, and New York) and abroad (Korea and England). He developed a knack for instruction and training, becoming a master instructor in charge of a 500-member squadron and, ultimately, a superintendent of training.

"I wanted to learn things and learn them fast, so I took every course available to me and learned how to relate to and manage people. The air force taught me about management," recalled McIntyre. As the oldest of four children reared by a single mother, McIntyre already knew a little bit about management and being responsible for others: "I was the oldest, so I didn't have a choice but to learn responsibility." McIntyre grew up just north of the Florida Panhandle in Brewton, Alabama. "I left home at fifteen years old to attending a boarding school, where I had a scholarship and worked to pay my way. It was a self-contained school, so you lived on campus, and we did farm work, grew crops, did carpentry work and landscaping. I was always working hard."

Equipped with this understanding about the importance of education and hard work for personal development, McIntyre found a good home in the air force, where he could apply his lessons and work ethic. In his spare time, McIntyre coached his station's women's basketball team to a few air force championship games.

As McIntyre approached the twenty-year mark in his military career, he started thinking about a second line of work. He had always been a fan of writing, having written for his high school newspaper and other publications over the years, and so decided he would pursue a new field: public affairs. His initial assignment was to help build the first public-affairs department for a special operations unit in Europe.

Three years later, he was working in New York under the secretary of the air force, handling national media and the military branches' ties to corporate America. In this capacity, McIntyre also helped promote the air force's art program, which sought to place air-force-themed artwork in museums and other exhibits. His biggest accomplishment came when an exhibit was displayed at the Empire State Building. It was so well received that the building's managers allowed him to have his retirement ceremony on the roof. McIntyre had made it to the top, it seemed, by stepping up for good causes.

After earning his master's in human resources from Saint Joseph's University in Philadelphia and becoming a grandfather, McIntyre joined FEMA, hoping to continue his career serving the public. FEMA, he says, was the perfect place for him to use all the experience gained during his air force career. "When 9/11 happened, I thought to myself, 'All the training, everything from knowledge of our military response to disaster response, came together in one day,'" said McIntyre, who now oversees disaster operations and workforce training for FEMA's public-affairs office. "FEMA gave me a chance to take what I know and be in a position to, hopefully, make the agency and others around me better."

What McIntyre is trying to do in his profession isn't all that different from what was accomplished by his role models, Dr. Martin Luther King, Jr., and former secretary of state Colin Powell. "Obviously, like a lot of young men growing up in the South, Martin Luther King was my role model. I remember thinking, the day he was assassinated, that I wanted to carry on his mission and that led me to want a career [in public service]," said McIntyre, whose two children live in Alabama.

"I had the opportunity to meet Colin Powell while I was stationed in North Dakota, and I was very impressed with how he carried himself," recalled McIntyre. "He was his own person, and I thought to myself, 'If I can be one ounce of that man, I'd be all right.'"

When it comes to personal difficulties, they say the most important part of solving a problem is to admit that you have one. Likewise, when it comes to public service, it appears the most important part of making a difference in the world is to acknowledge that you can. McIntyre has moved far past acknowledgment and is squarely focused on making a difference. McIntyre added, "I have a desire to make an impact, not just be present, but have an impact on my community, my country, and the people around me. I want to touch someone's life and know that they're better because of that touch."

CHAPTER 9

Tracie Hall

ASSISTANT DEAN AND LIBRARIAN AT
DOMINICAN UNIVERSITY

There are two things you need to know about Tracie Hall. First, she is a librarian. Second, she wants to change the world. Pair those two things together, and you have the making of a real role model.

Following in the footsteps of Martin Luther King, Hall is taking heed to Gandhi's words by being the change she wishes to see in the world. While Gandhi and King were national voices for widespread social change, Hall is taking a much different, and perhaps more novel, approach to making the world a better place. "I want to use a library as a vehicle to change the world, one community at a time," said Hall, assistant dean of Dominican University's Graduate School of Library and Information Sciences.

At Dominican, just outside Chicago, Hall is responsible for admissions, fundraising, marketing, and recruiting for one of the nation's premier graduate schools for aspiring library professionals. Interestingly, Hall didn't grow up wanting to become a librarian, much less a university administrator. Instead, it took time for her to discover a profession that combined her love of community involvement, interaction, and research.

In fact, it is unlikely anyone growing up in South Central Los Angeles, especially in the years leading up to the LA riots, would have envisioned herself as a librarian. Hall, however, didn't let the murder of her eldest brother, along with the near-death experiences of her other two brothers, prevent her from making something of herself.

Hall left South Central to attend college at the University of California, Santa Barbara, earning two degrees: one in law and society and another in black studies. The latter allowed her to move to Africa and take classes at Kenya's University of Nairobi for a school year.

In Africa, far away from the comforts and privileges of American life, Hall discovered the true importance of libraries. "In Kenya, I realized there was this scarcity of information and that access to information was a privilege," said Hall, who went on to earn a master's degree in African studies from Yale. "[In Kenya] I couldn't just go to a bookstore and buy a book. Sometimes you would have to get a book and copy it by hand, since there were no copy machines. It made me realize how important access to information is. That was when the seed [to become a librarian] was planted." While at Yale, Hall was able to study in some of the nation's best libraries, and that, coupled with her experiences in Kenya, drove her to make the library an important part of everything she did from that point on.

Although Hall was greatly inspired by the challenges and opportunities she encountered in Nairobi, she remembered what it had been like in South Central, and she always envisioned finding a way to give back to the community she had worked so hard to make it out of. Eventually, she returned to Southern California, where she became a project director for a homeless shelter. She managed a staff of case managers, oversaw a youth crisis shelter, and helped children and teens make the transition from temporary emergency shelters to longer-term homes.

The children's unfamiliarity with libraries appalled her. Many of them did not understand the concept of getting a library card, borrowing a book, or returning it at their convenience. She set out to educate her community about how easy—and important—it was to use the public library.

Hall soon found herself moving up the West Coast to Seattle, where she began working for the Seattle Public Library. Because of her experience working with youth, Hall was called upon to handle young-adult materials for one of the key branches, where she founded a youth camp and a creative-writing program for students. For her efforts in Seattle, Hall was honored by the mayor and by the American Library Association, which gave her its "Innovative Service to Young Adults" award.

After completing her master's in library and information science at the University of Washington, Hall was summoned back to the East Coast. She had decided to take the plunge and become a full-fledged librarian. Her first assignment was in New Haven, Connecticut, the home of Yale University and a small city with its share of social challenges, including high rates of HIV infection and drug use. She was a young-adult librarian charged with reaching out to teens through after-school programs, community centers, and juvenile detention centers.

While in New Haven, Hall also taught Swahili language courses (she is fluent) at Wesleyan University and gender studies lessons at Southern Connecticut State University. Whenever and wherever possible, Hall shared her knowledge like an open book. However, it was in the library that she made her greatest impact in the community.

In 2000, Hall joined the Hartford Public Library system to run its Albany branch, which had not been a pillar of the community. But that all changed quickly. While managing the branch's collection and circulation aspects, Hall routinely lobbied for resources to improve the appearance and function of her branch. To reach out to members of the community, she joined several school and community-related organizations and advisory boards; this allowed her to increase awareness and familiarity of the library within the community.

"At first, parents wouldn't come in, because of the terrible appearance of the library. They basically used the library as a temporary babysitter for the time between their kids leaving school and when they got off work," said Hall. Ultimately, thanks to Hall's stewardship, parents came to enjoy the library along with their children, and recognition soon followed. Hartford mayor Eddie Perez designated February 13 "Tracie Hall Day" to acknowledge her selfless and tireless efforts to improve the community by improving the local library.

In 2003, Hall was offered the opportunity to run the American Library Association's Office of Diversity. One of her brightest professional moments came when a Hartford resident found out about her approaching departure to take the new position, which was in Chicago, halfway across the country. "This man found out I was leaving Hartford and he said, 'You've made us pregnant, now you're leaving.' That's probably the best compliment I have ever received," said Hall.

As director of ALA's Office of Diversity, Hall was the national catalyst for diversity initiatives at libraries across the country. She was responsible for developing programs, training, raising funds for new campaigns, and publishing the ALA's diversity periodical, *Versed,* which reaches librarians around the country. Just one year into the job, Hall was named a "Mover and Shaker" by *Library Journal* magazine.

Though she started out in South Central with no idea of becoming a librarian, Hall now focuses most of her time on helping young adults become librarians. Fittingly, she also runs an information and nonprofit management company that goes by the name of the GoodSeed Group.

Sure enough, Tracie Hall is planting those seeds for a better world—one seed, one library, and one community at a time.

CHAPTER 10

Civil Rights and Real Role Models

Along with the black journalists and TV personalities like Oprah Winfrey and ESPN's Stuart Scott, who have inspired millions, there are others, outside of the people we regularly interact with, whom we look to as role models. Some derive encouragement from Harriet Tubman, who helped others escape slavery along the Underground Railroad; others might see an example in entrepreneur and early hip-hop pioneer Russell Simmons, whose Def Jam Recordings promoted the careers of artists like LL Cool J and Jay-Z. But if, by definition, a real role model acknowledges his or her ability to positively influence others, there was no better period for role models than the years of the civil rights movement. This chapter offers a brief history of some of the people who paved the way for those profiled in this book.

From the mid-1950s to the early 1970s, these role models were everywhere, it seemed. They were conducting sit-ins at lunch counters, boycotting bus systems, spreading love, and deflecting hate, which sometimes came as a spray from a high-pressure water hose or an attack by police dogs. Whether they were being arrested, beaten, or spat on, they valued the cause of equality higher than their personal pride. They wanted what all Americans want, what the Declaration of Independence promises them: life, liberty, and the pursuit of happiness.

Those promises, however, were denied them by whites, and

it took years—from Tubman's escape in 1849 to the Supreme Court's decision in *Brown v. Board of Education* in 1954—simply to prime America for a full-scale campaign to secure those God-given rights. Fortunately, there were plenty of role models—both on the national scale and in communities across the nation—willing to step up and contribute.

In 1944, a black man named Jackie Robinson refused to move to the back of an army bus while stationed at Fort Hood, Texas. Three years later, Robinson became the first black to play baseball in the major leagues. He endured intense prejudice and racism throughout his first season, but was still named that year's top new player. In 1962, he was inducted into the Baseball Hall of Fame, enshrined alongside Babe Ruth and other greats.

Following his storied career, Robinson joined the board of directors of the National Association for the Advancement of Colored People (NAACP) and often used his fame to help blacks who were being denied opportunities.

Around the same time that Robinson's Brooklyn Dodgers were becoming perennial World Series contenders, a successful trial lawyer named Thurgood Marshall, who was serving as chief counsel for the NAACP, appeared before an all-white U.S. Supreme Court to argue against school segregation in a case styled *Brown vs. Board of Education*. On May 17, 1954, the Supreme Court agreed unanimously with Marshall that the "separate but equal" doctrine was unconstitutional when applied to public schools. In 1967, Marshall became the first black justice on the Supreme Court.

Not long after Marshall argued *Brown* before the Court, a black seamstress took a seat on a bus after a long day at work. Earlier in her life, Rosa Parks had attempted to go to college and become a teacher—one of the few professions open to black women at the time—but was forced to leave when her grandmother and mother became ill. Instead, Parks worked at a department store and spent her spare time supporting the

NAACP in Montgomery, Alabama. On December 1, 1955, her refusal to give up her seat to a white man made her a major figure in the civil rights movement. Her actions helped put an end to segregation not only in Alabama, but throughout the nation.

Parks's refusal sparked a boycott of the Montgomery bus system, and a local pastor named Dr. Martin Luther King, Jr., only twenty-six years old at the time, was designated to lead the protest. Over the 381 days of boycotting, from December 5, 1955, to December 20, 1956, King rose to national prominence, and he used his influence to create the Southern Christian Leadership Conference (SCLC). As head of that group, King became the most widely known and well-respected leader of the civil rights movement for the next decade.

His "I Have a Dream" speech, which drew thousands to Washington's Lincoln Memorial, stands as one of the greatest speeches in American history, alongside Abraham Lincoln's Gettysburg Address, which repeated the call for equality for all Americans a full century earlier.

In 1965, King described the recently assassinated Malcolm X this way: "While we did not always see eye to eye on methods to solve the race problem, I always had a deep affection for Malcolm and felt that he had a great ability to put his finger on the existence and the root of the problem. He was an eloquent spokesman for his point of view and no one can honestly doubt that Malcolm had a great concern for the problems we face as a race."

Malcolm X played a significant role in the civil rights movement, largely through his leadership position in the Nation of Islam. He is credited with leading world-champion boxer Cassius Clay to the Muslim faith and encouraging him to change his name to Muhammad Ali. Ali became one of the greatest and most outspoken athletes of all time.

In 1962, James Meredith became the first black student to enroll in the University of Mississippi. His safety had to be ensured by federal troops and U.S. Marshals sent by President John F. Kennedy. Four years later, Meredith attempted to lead a walk into unfriendly territory again, this time marching from Memphis, Tennessee, to Jackson, Mississippi. He was nearly fatally shot by a sniper. Along with King, Stokely Carmichael took up Meredith's march. Carmichael was chairman of the Student Nonviolent Coordinating Committee (SNCC), a key organization for young people supporting the civil rights movement. Carmichael was arrested while marching; he later became a national icon by becoming the champion of the term "black power."

Andrew Young was even more deeply rooted in the politics of the civil rights era. As a fellow Alabama pastor, Young became a leading supporter and friend of King while serving as executive director of the SCLC. In the years after King's death, Young was elected to Congress, became the first black U.S. ambassador to the United Nations, served as mayor of Atlanta, and was an instrumental member of the group that secured the 1996 Olympics for that city. By then, Atlanta and much of the South had come a long way since Young and others were deeply entrenched in a fight for basic civil rights.

And there are others who stand out for their contributions to the civil rights movement: A. Philip Randolph helped gain significant employment rights for black workers; Ella Baker was a lifelong civil rights advocate and source of wisdom; Ralph Abernathy and Fred Shuttlesworth cofounded the SCLC with King; and Huey Newton and Bobby Seale started the Black Panther Party, which offered a more aggressive side to the movement.

The civil rights movement should be remembered for these and other leaders—not because they were perfect, since all of the people mentioned above had their share of lapses and shortcomings, but because each of them served as a role model within the movement.

Today there are still several civil rights activists, many of whom were active in King's lifetime, but the torch has been passed from King and the other leaders not to these individuals alone, but more broadly to all of us. President Obama would likely agree with this statement. While the type of activism made popular during the civil rights movement is not as visible today—much of that work is now done in legislatures and courts—it remains a significant element in telling the story of our history and shaping our future.

And for the profiles in this book, we did not want to highlight people who have sought simply to mirror what black leaders did in the past. Instead, we feature those who have taken new paths to becoming leaders and role models for black Americans. Many of these people are too young to have been active during the movement, and some are too young to have heard King give that memorable speech, but they are certainly marching on, just like Stokely Carmichael and others.

Their marches have led them to find new ways to make a difference and pave the way for the next generation, which will include doctors, scientists, business executives, and educators.

These are the torchbearers of Dr. King's dream.

CHAPTER 11

Kimberlydawn Wisdom, MD

SURGEON GENERAL OF THE STATE OF MICHIGAN

Talk to Dr. Kimberlydawn Wisdom, and you will quickly sense what is important to her: improving the community. "I want the ability to be at the table and have a voice," said Wisdom, who, as Michigan's surgeon general, became the first black person to serve as the chief public-health officer of any state. "I'm always thinking about how I can best serve the community," she added. After more than five years in a job that puts her in a position to revitalize Michigan's public health system, Wisdom is definitely at the table and making a difference in the community.

As part of her job, Wisdom has traveled throughout Michigan, meeting with thousands of residents, doctors, political figures, business leaders, teachers, and researchers to figure out how to improve the state's health from top to bottom. Her many public-health initiatives have sparked interest from others who have heard her on ABC's *Nightline* and the Food Network as well as at conferences put on by the National Governors Association and the Congressional Black Caucus.

The surgeon general's job, she said, is a natural fit because it allows her to draw on many of her experiences and interests from more than twenty years as a practicing physician, researcher, and educator.

But Wisdom's experiences and interests in the medical field date back much further. She initially became interested in medicine as a seven-year-old after seeing her mother, often ill with asthma and migraines, navigate the health system during the 1960s while they were living in a small Connecticut town about halfway between New York and Boston. "I had a lot of passion for addressing racial issues in health care, and felt I could make a contribution [as a doctor]," said Wisdom. "I had an interest in science and math in school. And my parents constantly supported and nurtured me." Wisdom got plenty of support from outside sources as well, including teachers, counselors, and community leaders. She even got to meet one of the most respected women of the civil rights era, Dr. Dorothy Height.

Wisdom became a young activist when she felt she had been mistreated at a YWCA camp, an incident that led to the energetic and engaged fourteen-year-old meeting Height, one of the leading social activists in the country. "I admired Dorothy Height for her commitment to the [civil rights] movement, her success in moving it forward, and her willingness and ability to engage someone," said Wisdom. "I liked the path she took to reach her goals, and she was willing to extend herself and didn't discount youth. She took my energy and helped channel it. It was not only what she did, but how she did it. It was something I wanted to emulate." And over the years, Wisdom has done a tremendous job of emulating Height's willingness to help others.

After graduating from the University of Pennsylvania with a bachelor's degree in biology (premed), Wisdom went on to medical school at the University of Michigan, one of the top public universities in the nation. She completed her medical residency at the Henry Ford Health System in Detroit and has stayed in Michigan ever since. While at Henry Ford, one of the busiest hospitals in the region, she considered a career as either a pediatric or an emergency-room physician. Ultimately, she settled on emergency medicine as her specialty. "I liked the pace [of the emergency room] and the different cases that came in," said Wisdom. "I like addressing the most critical needs. It's challenging, stimulating, and gratifying."

Wisdom went on to pick up a master's degree from the University of Michigan's public health school, and then began her life's work of focusing on preventive medicine and encouraging healthy lifestyles and habits. In her job, she works to close racial and socioeconomic gaps in health-care availability and treatment.

She has spent many years working to help people make better health choices, such as planning for pregnancy, and to prevent chronic illnesses and diseases, like diabetes, that have plagued the black community. She is currently spearheading a healthy-living campaign called Michigan Steps Up, which guides people through a plan to improve their health through exercise, better eating, and not smoking. In addition, she founded and has directed the Institute of Multicultural Health at Henry Ford and an award-winning community-based health-screening initiative called AIMHI (African American Initiative for Male Health Improvement), which works to improve the health of black men.

And as if all these projects didn't keep her busy enough, she is also an assistant professor of medical education at the University of Michigan Medical Center and serves as an adjunct assistant professor in the Department of Health Behavior and Health Education at the University of Michigan School of Public Health. For her efforts, she received an honorary doctorate from the Morehouse School of Medicine, in Atlanta.

Today, Wisdom has a right to be proud of where she is, given that she started with the goal of only becoming a doctor. "I didn't know all of the possibilities," said Wisdom. "Being a doctor is a privilege, and medicine is an honorable profession where I can serve my community. As I became more involved and developed an expertise, I thought I could take it to the next level."

From her many accomplishments and endeavors, it is clear

Wisdom has done just that. Years ago, she realized it was important to have a seat at the table and be in a position to have her voice heard. Today, she has the ear of the governor of Michigan, college students at a leading university, and patients. Her life's path can serve as a how-to for those interested in helping their own communities.

CHAPTER 12

Timothy George, MD

CHIEF OF PEDIATRIC NEUROSCIENCE AT DELL
CHILDREN'S MEDICAL CENTER

The Dell Children's Medical Center in Austin, Texas, is a long way from the tough streets of Bedford-Stuyvesant in Brooklyn, New York. There, Dr. Timothy George said it was often "do or die in Bed-Stuy." To survive, George had a group of friends he relied on, but it was far from a gang.

He believes the difference between himself today and the kids he grew up with lies not in his talent, skill, intellectual ability, or sense of community, but in the direction he embraced. George and his childhood friends stood together, committed to doing something special in order to make it. They knew that a sense of closeness, respect, and unity was the way to survive the streets of Brooklyn and protect one another. But most importantly, they stood together to make a positive difference in the world. From that, George has gone on to do plenty of difference-making all on his own.

George took that desire to make a difference from New York City to Durham, North Carolina, and the Duke University Medical School, where he was a tenured professor of neurosurgery. From there, he moved to the Dell Children's Medical Center in Austin, Texas, where he presently serves as chief of service of the Pediatric Neurosurgery Center of Central Texas and as an adjunct professor of cellular microbiology at the University of Texas.

Reflecting on his childhood, George remembers wanting to

do something to help people. He was always fascinated with science, and the human body in particular, but admits that it was a long time before he connected that fascination with becoming a physician. He didn't know any physicians except the one he went to when he was sick, so he had no role models in that profession. The only way to figure out how to become a doctor was to go out and educate himself on the subject.

George remembers having to decide, like most of the kids in his neighborhood, between playing ball to fit in or fighting to be tough. He was better at playing ball, often as a point guard, and that experience taught him that his true skills were those of a leader. He noticed that when he talked, people listened, and he knew that if people were going to follow him, he had better lead them in the right direction, whether it was to victory on the court or doing the right thing in the neighborhood.

Learning to lead in the right direction appeared to derive from his father, whom, George stated, is one of his heroes. Though his father, a plumber, had only an eighth-grade education, he took care of not only pipes, but also people's needs. George recalled how his father would look after the well-being of the guys who worked for him. Many times he would work into the evenings or on weekend jobs to help provide extra money for his workers so they could provide for their own children.

Another hero of George's was Muhammad Ali, whom he admired for the flair with which he took on opponents in the ring and his unwavering willingness to stand up for what he believed was right. He also held the activist-comedian Dick Gregory in high esteem for his courage to talk about the problems of the world in a way that could empower people while challenging those who were powerful.

George views education as the way to make it in the world. The purpose of education, according to him, is to "train your mind" and to "learn how to think" rather than just to get a job. He knows that education is the only tool that can change and empower those willing to learn to use it. An important benefit of education is gaining self-confidence. George advises young people to "never quit!" He explains that failing does not mean that you are a failure; it means you have to work harder and smarter to accomplish to accomplish your goals. It takes confidence to believe that you can do it.

His admiration for black people cuts to the core of one of his most heartfelt convictions. He sincerely believes that blacks have contributed to this country and the world in countless ways besides sport and entertainment. Black people are be valuable in all areas of society and should not put limitations on themselves. Blacks, George said, "should be presidents, CEOs, even neurosurgeons. There is nothing we shouldn't do."

His interest in pediatrics was sparked in high school, when he had the opportunity to work with disabled children. He quickly realized that there were kids with problems far worse than his.

George's interest in science led him to attend college. He felt fortunate to be recruited by several universities to play basketball, but he decided to attend Columbia University, mainly because others said he couldn't get in. At Columbia, he was profoundly challenged by an environment that was vastly different from the his upbringing. Both the people and their mindsets were different. His self-worth was challenged as he went to class with people from families worth millions of dollars and thought being at Columbia was simply a rite of passage. Later, in medical school at New York University, he was challenged by conservative professors whose personalities were often militaristic. These types of people were also on the faculty at Duke Medical School.

Through all the challenges, George learned something about himself: to be persistent and consistent. His "never give up" attitude sustained him through the rigorous educational process required of a doctor. He admits that he was often nervous when confronting a new school, training, or leadership position, but the nerves gave way as he learned to be cool and calm under pressure. Early on he was often self-protective and never let people see beyond the facade, which he thought he needed to survive. As he became more confident, he was able to unveil the true person inside to others.

George seems to personify the meaning of his favorite quote: "What we're saying today is that you're either part of the solution or you're part of the problem" (civil rights leader Eldridge Cleaver, San Francisco, 1968). When it comes to children's health, Dr. Timothy George is certainly a huge part of the solution.

CHAPTER 13

Victoria Holloway Barbosa, MD

ETHNIC DERMATOLOGIST AND FORMER EXECUTIVE FOR L'OREAL

We have all been asked the question: What do you want to be when you grow up? None of us can go back to first grade and answer that question again, but we should take heed of how Victoria Holloway Barbosa made sure her answer didn't fall by the wayside as she got older. "I've always wanted to be a doctor since I was six," said Dr. Barbosa. "I never wavered from that. I loved my pediatrician, and I didn't like going to the doctor's office, but I loved his office and the stickers he gave me. His name was Dr. Holman."

Dr. Holman isn't around to take credit for inspiring Barbosa, but she knows he was the first physician she had as a role model. And over the years, especially during all those years in school, Barbosa surely spent a moment or two recalling those childhood visits to the doctor's office and remembering why she decided to become a doctor. Today, Barbosa is a board-certified physician specializing in dermatology, with patients ranging from teens to senior citizens. You can be sure she serves each one with the care that a doctor would give a nervous child, because she knows that, on any given day, a future doctor could be in her office.

But before she was a doctor, she was a student. And as any doctor will tell you, you have to enjoy school if you want to become a doctor some day. Fortunately for Barbosa, her mother was a guidance counselor who gave her nothing but encouragement to pursue her medical ambitions. "My mother being a guidance counselor came in handy, but she didn't have to push me," said Barbosa. "I always had that internal drive, and my mother and family nurtured my strengths and told me I could do anything. I always believed that everything was possible."

With such a supportive environment, Barbosa was able to perform well in school while volunteering at the local hospital in her hometown of White Plains, New York. She loved being in a hospital, and her desire to become a doctor only grew. Soon, she was a biology major at Harvard University. She said she thinks of her days at Harvard as a time when she combined her intellect with her intuition.

Her intelligence and instinct certainly come in handy later at medical school at Yale University. It was there she had to decide what kind of doctor she would become. After graduating with honors, she settled on dermatology. "I felt that my service to the community could be fulfilled through my profession," said Barbosa. "I thought [about dermatology] because skin and hair is a way that we, as black people, define ourselves culturally."

She would go on to complete an internship in internal medicine at Massachusetts General Hospital, a high-profile hospital where she was "taught what it is to be a doctor." She later served as a dermatology resident at Yale–New Haven Hospital, where she also functioned as chief resident.

But she wasn't finished with school. She accepted an offer to be a Robert Wood Johnson Clinical Scholar at Johns Hopkins University School of Medicine, one of the most esteemed medical institutions in the world. While at Johns Hopkins, she also picked up a master's degree in public health. "I liked school, and I felt like it was a privilege," said Barbosa. "You create some of your blessings, and [by going to Johns Hopkins] I felt like my whole world of opportunity broadened. I could do research at an academic medical center or have a private practice. When I finished school, I told my mother that I wanted to run something."

And Barbosa was able to do exactly what she said she would. By a stroke of good luck and thanks to her hard work, in 2003 Barbosa was offered the chance to create and run the Institute for Ethnic Hair and Skin Research at L'Oreal, a leading cosmetics manufacturer, in Chicago, after working for the company for three years. In this role, she managed a staff of physicians, chemists, and biologists who did basic research to discover the unique qualities of the hair and skin of people of African descent. In her position at L'Oreal, Barbosa helped create and expand the field of ethnic dermatology. This is fitting, since black patients so often seek her out because there are so few black dermatologists.

"I love being a doctor because that's part of my core," said Barbosa. "But being in research is great because when you're a doctor, you're seeing one person at a time versus potentially impacting millions with research. So [with research], I felt like my reach was greater and it was more challenging."

After seven years, Barbosa left her job with L'Oreal to spend more time with patients and teach at the Rush University Medical Center Department of Dermatology, in Chicago. She also started her own business, Dermal Insights, Inc., a company providing education, inspirational lectures, and consulting services. Stepping out on her own probably wasn't much of a risk. After all, she is considered a leader in the field of ethnic dermatology and chaired the International Ethnic Hair and Skin Research Symposia sponsored by L'Oreal. She is a member of the American Association for the Advancement of Science's Committee on Opportunities in Science and a founding board member of the Skin of Color Society. She even picked up a master of business administration degree at Northwestern University's Kellogg School of Business.

Four degrees from prestigious universities and experience both as a doctor and researcher make Barbosa a very successful person. "I love reaching people, public speaking, and sharing experiences," said Barbosa. "But there is no greater privilege than having someone entrust their health with you."

But it is not just her career that makes her a real role model: it is also her willingness and desire to help others. She encourages young people to seek ways to serve others as well. "You have to live as though you're a role model even if you're not. If you strive to be helpful and compassionate and serve others, you don't have to be a physician to be a role model," said Barbosa. "Most role models are people you come into contact with every day." You may not visit a doctor that often, but Dr. Victoria Holloway Barbosa's success story is one worth checking into regularly.

CHAPTER 14

Bill Douglas

WHITE HOUSE CORRESPONDENT FOR
MCCLATCHY NEWSPAPERS

As we have seen, blacks since the civil rights era have made a big impact in the worlds of public service and medicine. They have also taken leading roles as media professionals. Here is a brief history of blacks in American journalism:

In 1961, Dorothy Gilliam became the first black female reporter hired by the *Washington Post*. Both before and during Gilliam's hiring, the media played a large role in helping Martin Luther King and his supporters demonstrate against the widespread racism in the country. In 1969, *Ebony* magazine photographer Moneta Sleet, Jr., became the first black man to win a Pulitzer Prize, for his shot of Dr. King's wife and son at his funeral.

In 1975, forty-four journalists formed the National Association of Black Journalists (NABJ) and named Chuck Stone, a reporter for the *Philadelphia Daily News,* its first president. More of America's newsrooms became open to blacks with each passing year. In 1978, ABC made Max Robinson the first black journalist to serve as a nightly news anchor for a major network.

In 1980, Robert Johnson formed Black Entertainment Television, making it the first black-owned national cable TV network in America. In 1981, Ed Bradley started his Emmy-winning career on *60 Minutes*. The next year, Bryant Gumbel became coanchor of *The Today Show* on NBC, the first black host of a network morning news show. In 1983, Robert Maynard became the first black man to own a major metropolitan newspaper when he took over the *Oakland Tribune*.

In 1993, Bob Herbert became the first black full-time columnist for the *New York Times*. In 1998, Mark Whitaker became the first black editor for a major newsweekly (*Newsweek*).

In 2002, Gregory Moore was named editor of the *Denver Post*, one of the top ten newspapers in the nation.

And there have been other major achievements for blacks in the media. Dick Parsons is chief executive for Time Warner, one of the most respected and successful media holding companies in the country. Robin Roberts and others have gained fame as sportscasters for ESPN and other networks, and Oprah Winfrey is perhaps the biggest name in all of television.

Black journalists also report the news from Wall Street, the war in Iraq, and the White House. Bill Douglas is among the last group.

Not too long ago, black journalists were not among those covering presidential matters. Imagine the president never having to answer a question from a black reporter. Today, Douglas is the White House correspondent for the McClatchy newspapers, which include, among a dozen daily publications around the country, the *Miami Herald, Kansas City Star,* and *Charlotte Observer*. Douglas's stories are often written from his Washington, D.C., office, but they end up on doorsteps everywhere from California to the Carolinas.

That isn't bad considering how he started his journalism career. His mother was a schoolteacher, and his father was in the navy, eventually rising to the rank of chief petty officer, so Douglas moved around a bit during his early childhood. He spent his formative years in the Philadelphia area. Even though his parents had fairly conventional jobs, Douglas described them as being very unconventional, mainly in giving him a diverse education. Little did they know that this unorthodox schooling would help Douglas prepare for his future profession in journalism.

Over the years, Douglas went to parochial, public, and private schools. He started in Catholic school, but he grew up at a time when being left-handed was frowned upon, and when he wasn't willing to become right-handed, Catholic school turned out not to be the right fit. Eventually, he attended a private school where he was one of fewer than two hundred students and the teaching methods were experimental. In fact, Douglas realized that there weren't many other black students for that reason. Again, his parents were far from conventional.

After high school, he went off to college, though he wasn't sure he was prepared for it. He decided to pursue a degree in journalism, a profession he had grown enamored with throughout his childhood. "The defining point in my life was when I was probably eight or nine years old and heard a typewriter," reflected Douglas. "I loved the sound of the typewriter, so I started writing little stories to myself. Eventually, I was writing articles, music reviews, letters to public officials. I wrote in the high school paper and the community paper, which was good, because it also got me free concert tickets when I did reviews."

Before starting college, Douglas was introduced to a Philadelphia journalism legend. Acel Moore, who retired in 2005 after forty-three years with the *Philadelphia Inquirer,* started out as a copy boy for the paper and rose to become a Pulitzer Prize winner. He also helped form the NABJ, which Douglas is now a member of, along with more than three thousand others. "Acel made it look so easy," recalled Douglas.

Douglas set off for the University of South Carolina in Columbia. "They had a pretty good journalism program, but part of the reason was because my grandparents were there and they were my safety valve in case I couldn't cut it," said Douglas. "Back then, if you were black, the professions you chose were to teach, work in the post office, be a nurse, or join the military. It wasn't really a guarantee that I'd make it in journalism." But he did make it, and in 1980 he set off on a lengthy career as a reporter.

Just a few years earlier, Douglas had seen then-president Jimmy Carter and realized that journalism was a way to "ask big people questions." After interning at the *Philadelphia Bullet* and *Greenville (S.C.) News* during college, Douglas got a job at the *Charlotte Observer*. After three years in Charlotte, Douglas moved to Atlanta, working at the *Journal-Constitution*, and later to Baltimore, where he met his wife and worked at the *Sun*. He covered police and education issues; if you have seen HBO's *The Wire*, you may be familiar with the issues facing both that city and the journalism business.

After building a strong portfolio and track record, Douglas landed in Brooklyn, New York, at *Newsday*, one of the most-read newspapers in the nation. He stayed with the paper for sixteen years, covering stories both in New York and Washington. During his time there, he reported on happenings in the New York City public schools, the mid-nineties Republican takeover of Congress, and President Clinton's second term. He earned his way into the White House press corps, traveling with and reporting on the president daily.

Douglas left the White House reporting gig to cover the Pentagon, but returned a few years later, this time during President George W. Bush's second term, just in time to ask big people questions about the Iraq War and the Hurricane Katrina fiasco. An avid hockey player, Douglas played weekly games with the man Bush defeated in 2004, Senator John Kerry.

Over his twenty-five-plus years in professional journalism, Douglas has lived by one of the principles he was taught by his father. "I always learned by trying and applying. The way my dad taught me to swim was by throwing me in the water," said Douglas. "I always learned that you go out and you do. So growing up, there was a little bit of that throwing yourself in the deep end. But you always try, and if you fail, you reapply, because you don't know what you can or can't do until you try."

Douglas took his own advice one year and invited President Clinton to his home for dinner. To his surprise, the president accepted, and Douglas and a few other black reporters had a home-cooked meal with the commander-in-chief. "Media is like a de facto family. There's camaraderie, but there's also competitiveness," said Douglas. Not long ago, Douglas wouldn't have had the chance even to compete for the chance to report from the White House. Now he is not only reporting on the president, he has shared a meal with one.

CHAPTER 15

Leonard Pitts, Jr.

COLUMNIST FOR THE *MIAMI HERALD*

Plenty of young adults can name someone who has won an Oscar or a Grammy Award. Fewer can name a Pulitzer Prize winner. Well, here is one Pulitzer Prize winner to remember: Leonard Pitts, Jr.

However, Pitts didn't need to win the equivalent of his profession's Oscar or Grammy to be considered a success. His words have already earned him that right. In fact, as a nationally syndicated columnist for the *Miami Herald,* Pitts reaches millions of readers every time he writes.

If Pitts's definition of a role model is accurate—"somebody who models desirable traits; things we'd like to emulate"—it is pretty easy to see why he is worthy of the designation. "My mom was my first and most important role model," said Pitts. "But I wanted to be a writer since I was five, and I grew up admiring [Spider-Man creator] Stan Lee and [children's author] Beverly Cleary."

Pitts grew up in South Central Los Angeles as a self-described nerdy kid in a dual-parent household that didn't exactly resemble the Cosbys. His father drank regularly, and his frequent unemployment required Pitts's family to move constantly. Pitts attended six different elementary schools.

As the oldest child, Pitts was instilled with a heightened sense of responsibility and was proud to help his stay-at-home mom around the house. One Christmas, he saved up enough money to help buy gifts for his younger brothers and sisters. Meanwhile, he was also working on his literary ambitions and started submitting works to local newspapers and magazines when he was twelve. Initially, Pitts fancied himself a poet who would be following in the footsteps of Langston Hughes; he published his first poem at fourteen in the *Los Angeles Sentinel*. "There's nothing like seeing your name in print for the first time," reflected Pitts. "Later on, I started to think that Maya Angelou was probably one of the few to make a living doing poetry, so I started looking at other ways to use my writing to have a career."

Pitts won a scholarship to the University of Southern California at fifteen. Not quite old enough to fully relate to and fit in with his older classmates, he focused much of his energy on his goals. By the time he was eighteen, he had earned a gig at *SOUL,* an LA-based black entertainment magazine.

During college, Pitts made a disheartening discovery. "I didn't realize until college that expectations were lower [for black students]," remembered Pitts. "My [white] roommate and I were talking about SAT scores, and I thought I did pretty well. He got a 1260 or something and I got a 1060 or something, but I remember my high school teachers talking like I was the smartest kid ever. I thought I was just as smart as my roommate, and I didn't just want to be compared to other black students. I wanted to compete against the best."

At nineteen, Pitts graduated college among the best, earning his English degree with high honors (summa cum laude). Still writing for *SOUL,* he spent two years reviewing music and interviewing established and up-and-coming black musicians. His talent shone, and he was named the magazine's editor before his twenty-first birthday.

Pitts interviewed the most famous black entertainers of the late 1970s and the 1980s, including Michael Jackson just before his first solo hit album, *Off the Wall,* hit stores. Over the years, Pitts interviewed legends like Marvin Gaye, the Temptations, Gladys Knight, and Lionel Richie.

As a freelancer, Pitts became a well-known music reviewer for *Reader's Digest, Spin, TV Guide,* and Los Angeles radio station KFWB. During this time of professional growth and success, Pitts also became a husband and father. Pitts is now the father of five, and many of his experiences as a father have fueled his writing.

Throughout the eighties, more avenues opened for to Pitts as a writer. After being the editor of a music program called *Radioscope,* he became a writer for radio pioneer Casey Kasem's *American Top 40* program. Also, he contributed scripts for award-winning documentaries about Dr. Martin Luther King, Jr. (*King: From Atlanta to the Mountaintop*) and other African Americans. Fittingly, one of Pitts's most memorable stories was written for the twentieth anniversary of King's assassination. He also remembers his stories on twentieth anniversaries of the assassination of Robert F. Kennedy and the death of rock 'n' roll legend Elvis Presley.

The most obvious quality of Pitts's career, from the beginning to the present day, has been his consistency. From one writing job to another, he has always kept dead aim at his childhood dream of being a professional writer. "A lot of people go to graduate school and study writing and learn techniques and all those things, but writers write," said Pitts, who is a member of the National Association of Black Journalists (NABJ). "You learn to write by writing. You have to practice the craft every day."

After a brief stint with popular radio company Westwood One as a music writer, Pitts became the music critic for the *Miami Herald.* Drawing on more than a decade of experience writing about music, Pitts used the position to showcase his expertise. In 1991, he won the National Headliner and American Association of Sunday and Feature Editors arts criticism awards, and the following year he was a Pulitzer Prize finalist.

In 1994, while attending a concert by legendary rock band U2, Pitts was attacked by a group of drunken white men, and his vivid and enthralling column about the assault raised his national profile tremendously. In 1995, he became a full-time columnist for the *Herald,* where he now writes about popular culture, race, and current events. Branching out from music and drawing on his fatherhood experiences, Pitts authored *Becoming Dad: Black Men and the Journey to Fatherhood,* for which he traveled to his father's childhood home in Mississippi and interviewed other black fathers.

In both 1994 and 1995, Pitts was honored by the NABJ as a premier commentary writer, and over the years he has racked up accolades and awards from the National Society of Newspaper Columnists, the Scripps Howard Foundation, the American Society of Newspaper Editors, *Editor and Publisher* magazine, and the Gay and Lesbian Alliance Against Defamation.

Pitts's column, which appears twice each week, is read by millions of Americans, and no column has resonated with more readers than his post-9/11 meditation titled, "We'll Go Forward From This Moment," which states: "As Americans we will weep, as Americans we will mourn, and as Americans, we will rise in defense of all that we cherish." He received nearly 30,000 e-mails after its initial appearance, and it has since been reprinted numerous times.

Pitts's success as a writer has given him a new platform and title: professor. In recent years, he has served as a visiting professor of journalism at Hampton University in Virginia, Ohio University, and Virginia Commonwealth University. "Writers are readers. When students tell me they love writing but they don't like reading, I have to remind them that if you want to be a writer, you need to be a reader," added Pitts. "Writers must be persistent and have inner direction to know where you want to get and the course you need to go to get there."

Pitts says he is a big fan of Stephen King, the best-selling author of *The Green Mile* and *Rita Hayworth and the Shaw-*

shank Redemption, and wants to write some fiction himself. Given Pitts's track record and his ability to stay focused on a goal, there is no reason to doubt that he could be a successful novelist.

In today's society, we cheer and praise actors who have five years of fame, singers who have two hit albums, and athletes who have ten-year careers. In that atmosphere of short-term accomplishment, Leonard Pitts, with his three decades of award-winning work, stands out as a real role model.

CHAPTER 16

Danyel Smith

When Danyel Smith sat down with actor Robert De Niro and rapper 50 Cent in 2008, it must have been a very special occasion. Officially, it was an interview to discuss *Righteous Kill*, a film De Niro and 50 had made together. But it was also a meeting of three successful professionals who have reached the top of their fields.

De Niro and 50, both native New Yorkers, honed their skills in their hometown. Smith, on the other hand, is originally from Oakland, California, but she made it to Manhattan by doing exactly what De Niro and 50 did: she rose to the top of her game. Today, Smith is editor in chief of *Vibe* magazine.

How Smith made it to the top of her profession starts with her childhood in California. First in Oakland and then in Los Angeles, she started out her writing career by keeping a journal and writing storybooks that she would enjoy reading. Over the years, she came to admire the literary styles of well-known female black authors like Terry McMillan, Toni Morrison, and Zora Neale Hurston. Still, even with those women as inspiration, Smith's own mother and other family and friends were the major role models during her childhood. Her mother and aunt were members of a club of black women who would spend time planning community events involving theatre, dance, and music. "I thought they were all very fabulous," Smith said of her mother and the other women. "They all had careers, and I wanted to be like them. They were having a good time being smart and beautiful at the same time."

Smith's mother also instilled some basic but much needed priorities in her young daughter: "stand up straight," "comb your hair," "graduate," "don't get pregnant," and "don't do drugs."

Her mother, a former insurance executive and now a preschool owner, also encouraged her to read the stories of women such as Mary McLeod Bethune and Harriet Tubman. Smith always thought that if those women could overcome whatever obstacles they encountered, then she could too. Another trailblazer for Smith was Cynthia Horner, who was the longtime editorial director for *Right On!* magazine. Smith told herself as a young writer that she, too, could become the editor of a successful magazine.

With those thoughts in mind, Smith headed to the University of California–Berkeley, one of the top public universities in the country. Unfortunately, family and financial problems overwhelmed Smith at college. She was once quoted for a *San Francisco Chronicle* article as saying, regarding her decision to drop out of college after three years, "At Cal, I was confused. I didn't have any guidance, and I didn't know how to fix my mouth to ask for any."

After taking some time to collect herself, Smith landed an internship at the *San Francisco Bay Guardian,* a city entertainment paper. She began exploring the growing hip-hop scene in the Bay Area. Finally, Smith found her niche. Very few people were writing about rap music during the early nineties, before rap became a global sensation, and she saw an opportunity. She began writing for the *San Francisco Weekly* and for *Rolling Stone* magazine before moving to New York and working for *Billboard* magazine and the *New York Times.*

In 1993, legendary music producer Quincy Jones started *Vibe,* and the following year, Smith was hired as its music editor. *Vibe* really wanted the young writer; she had just turned down the chance to be the magazine's West Coast editor in order to move to New York. At *Vibe,* Smith has written countless cover stories and has interviewed entertainment celebrities such as Whitney Houston, Janet Jackson, and Wesley Snipes.

Despite the excitement of helping to lead a growing magazine, Smith was determined to finish her education. She took a one-year leave of absence to study at Northwestern University's first-rate journalism school. She returned to *Vibe* as editor in chief in the aftermath of one of hip-hop's most trying times, the period after the shooting deaths of Tupac Shakur and the Notorious B.I.G. However, it was also a very successful time for the magazine, as circulation exceeded half a million readers under Smith's leadership.

Never one to settle into a job too easily, Smith left after two years to do some freelance writing, teach at the New School in New York, and start writing fiction. She published her first book, *More Like Wrestling,* in 2003. It is a story of two young women from her hometown of Oakland.

Teaching journalism students at the New School motivated Smith to go back to school once again, this time to complete a master of fine arts (MFA) degree.

"I don't like to not finish something," Smith said about dropping out of college the first time around. "Speaking in front of students, it was always something I felt was important for me to be able to tell students, 'Don't take that course.' Now it's a point of pride for me to have my MFA, and I can say that I went back and finished up [my education]."

It is admirable that Smith, even with all the professional success she had enjoyed, still understood the importance of completing her college education. Few people as established in their careers as she was at that point would have done the same. Her return to school was in line with her personal motto: "Do more than what's expected of me."

In 2006, she did something else that few would have expected: she returned to *Vibe* for a second stint as editor in chief. A 2006 interview for MediaBistro.com quoted Smith as saying, "It seems like I've always been with *Vibe*. It feels like I never left . . . I love *Vibe*." It seems as if *Vibe* magazine, not New York, is Smith's current residence. Smith has said many times that it is a great privilege to work for *Vibe,* even through the ups and downs and rigors of her job.

While De Niro had his best roles years ago and 50 Cent's rap career has been on the decline lately, Smith appears to still be on her way up from the top. When asked how she feels about where she is today in her life, she said she is happy, but never satisfied. "I think that's next week," Smith said about reaching her career's peak moment. "I don't ever want that moment . . ."

Even if that moment never arrives for Smith, she has already reached a position as a real role model. She encourages young blacks to be on the lookout for role models at home, in school, and in history. "Not everyone has good parents, but a lot [of people] do. Not every person has a great teacher, but a lot do. Look to coaches. Look to the classics and read *Their Eyes Were Watching God* and read about Harriet Tubman and Florence Nightingale," Smith said.

And if that's not enough, just follow Smith's simple advice: "be on time," "don't accept the first no," "don't lie," and "be independent." That kind of a advice isn't found in movies or rap lyrics, but it will certainly help you learn from Danyel Smith's story to reach the top of your game.

Author's note: As this book was going to press in the summer of 2009, Quincy Jones announced the magazine would shut down print operations in light of the recession. Vibe *maintains an online presence.*

CHAPTER 17

Are We Really "Keepin' It Real"?

So now that you have seen some examples of the kind of people we consider role models, let's talk a little bit about the other word in the title of this book: *real*. Just as it is important to address the need for role models within the black community, it is also important to address what it means to be real. We don't pretend to have an exact definition. *Real* is much too broad a concept; defining it would be like trying to define the word *fun*. Instead, we have relied heavily on our personal history with the word. Here is a little background.

During the mid to late 1990s, the word *real* was inescapable as part of the phrase "keepin' it real." For blacks in America, the phrase "keepin' it real" has had all types of implications and meanings, but for its prominence during the 1990s, when the phrase showed up in everything from music videos to magazine advertisements, we can credit hip-hop culture.

In the 1990s, hip-hop, and gangsta rap in particular, wove its way into all aspects of American pop culture, ushering in a new definition of what it meant to be real. For most of the '90s, when we were in school (one of us as a student, the other as a teacher), black kids enjoyed listening to the music of Tupac and the Notorious B.I.G. These and other popular rappers, we were repeatedly being told, knew what it meant to "keep it real."

On the surface, we can identify with some of the stories

told by hip-hop, since we grew up in households and neighborhoods not all that different from those of the rappers whose lyrics were frequently recited by our students and classmates. So sort of like the street hustlers turned rappers, we knew what it meant to have to earn every opportunity to make something of ourselves.

Still, when friends or students claimed to be "keepin' it real," we couldn't go along with the general understanding of the phrase. At that time, keepin' it real had little or nothing to do with being your own person and remaining true to yourself, which we both believed should be its true meaning. What is real is what is unique to each person. Instead, for many young blacks, keepin' it real had everything to do with cultural conformity and identifying with every aspect of hip-hop culture—that was how blacks were supposed to act.

This sentiment was echoed by celebrities like NBA all-star Allen Iverson, who was seen as the foremost hip-hop-era icon in professional sports. Iverson was the embodiment of how to keep it real, not because he remained true to himself, but because he acted the way people thought all young blacks were supposed to act, meaning he wore baggy clothes and flashy jewelry and even made a rap album.

In other words, black children were being told that keepin' it real wasn't about being who you really were deep down as much as it was about being the person others expected you to be . . . someone more like Allen Iverson. And during those years, plenty of young blacks took keepin' it real to mean they needed to identify with the criminality and street mentality of the rappers and actors they saw on TV.

Furrah Qureshi, a former Drexel University student, wrote about the implications of this in a 2007 article:

We're not just combating an economic issue; we have to combat a cultural issue . . .

It reminds me of a friend of mine who's currently in high school and is an African American male with eyes for Cornell and Harvard, he totes a report card of strictly A's and frequents theater classes and all anyone ever says to him is, "way to act white." I of course know, that this is a joke, but what sort of message is this joke sending? That being intelligent and well rounded is a "white" thing? If being white is supposed to mean being smart that what does being black mean?

None of this is meant to imply that Allen Iverson is not a real role model. In fact, Iverson has done tremendous things in his hometown of Newport News, Virginia, and in Philadelphia, where he played ten seasons for the NBA's Sixers. However, not every black role model carries him- or herself like Iverson, and it is a major problem to expect them to.

Throughout these pages, you will read about people who are a lot like Allen Iverson in that they have used their talents to make something of themselves and give back to their communities. However, they aren't necessarily the types to wear baggy clothes and thousands of dollars worth of jewelry. This should not be lead to any skepticism regarding their realness.

In fact, if keepin' it real means succeeding even though the odds are stacked against you, many of these people are about as real as it gets. This is because they had not only to deal with being one of the few blacks in their chosen professions, unlike NBA players, but also to handle the peer pressure to conform to other blacks' ideas of keepin' it real. Imagine a six-foot-something black teen who chose the science club over the basketball team.

Whether in their rough childhood neighborhoods or at college, they probably faced resistance from the black community itself when trying to succeed on their own terms. Blazing a trail is not always easy, but these people have in many ways tried to do just that.

There are probably millions of children who can identify

with Iverson and his life experiences and style. But it shouldn't be considered not real to identify with the life experiences and qualities of the black men and women who don't fit the hip-hop image yet are successful in their own right. This is not an attack on hip-hop, which we have listened to for years. This is simply a statement about how important it will continue to be for young black people to carve their own paths to success and remain true to themselves. Why? Because being real is different for everyone, but we can all be real role models just the same.

CHAPTER 18

Ed Stewart

VICE PRESIDENT OF CORPORATE COMMUNICATIONS
FOR TICKETMASTER

You have probably heard stories of NBA or NFL stars refusing to play until they were offered a higher-paying contract. In 2004, former NBA all-star Latrell Sprewell became infamous for refusing a salary of $7 million because he "had a family to feed." We are sure that as a high school basketball player, Sprewell never could have imagined being paid $7 million a year to play the game he loved, but once he made it to the NBA, he did what too many black professional athletes and celebrities do: he traded his passion for pay. Millions of young black children dream of being professional athletes. We can only hope that those who make it grow up to become role models—not because of their salaries, but because of their passion to play their sport, reach their potential, and give back to the community.

Because being a real role model isn't about being rich and famous, this book does not profile the forty wealthiest black professionals or America's top black celebrities. It is our full belief that a person's passion for what he or she does, not the money or fame that comes from doing it, makes that person a real role model.

Nearly every person we interviewed wanted to know the same thing: "What do the people you've met with have in common?" Passion for their life's work, we discovered, was one of the prime answers. The best way to prove the point was to tell them about Ed Stewart.

I (Spearman) came to know Stewart when I was twenty years old and had just been accepted for a summer internship in Southwest Airlines' public relations department, where he was the senior director. There were other people in charge of the internship program, but he definitely set the "work hard, play hard" tone for the entire office. During my summer there, it wasn't uncommon to hear Stewart say outrageous things to reporters, once calling himself "the one black guy surrounded by all these blondes." I soon learned that this was one of his tactics, which proved beneficial to Southwest when the company was in a heated battle with crosstown rival American Airlines. An employee for American once lamented that Southwest's CEO Gary Kelly was "just as annoying as their head spokesman, Ed Stewart. Thankfully, Ed took a job elsewhere."

That summer I learned Stewart was a person who truly had a passion for life and loved his work. And he was one of the first people I wanted to interview for this book, not simply because he was a successful black man in my chosen profession (I majored in public relations), but mostly because of his passion.

Passionate people inspire those around them to do a good job and to enjoy doing it. And as many successful people will confirm, when you enjoy your professional life, that enjoyment spreads easily to other aspects of your life. That was definitely true for me that summer. I got the chance to learn from one of the best, and make a lasting acquaintance, but also to understand how Southwest managed to be both a fun and friendly airline as well as a consistently successful company: it was because people like Ed Stewart were in positions to help others enjoy their work.

Stewart got his start in Milwaukee, Wisconsin, the oldest of four children. His parents owned a community grocery store, but his father also worked in real estate, and his mother helped at the local YWCA. However, Stewart knew from an early age that his energy was too much for just his community and that he wanted to work in the news business.

Milwaukee was one of the first cities with a black news anchor, and Stewart saw broadcast journalism as a way to reach people and make a difference. "I loved communication and the immediacy of [broadcast] journalism," said Stewart. "I liked the idea of being involved in something as it was unfolding."

After graduating from the University of Wisconsin, Stewart served as a general-assignment and political reporter for network-affiliate television stations in Milwaukee and Oklahoma City. He covered everything from local crime stories to U.S. presidents. And fittingly for a man who wanted to be a part of the story, Stewart's journalism career coincided with the rise of the kind of live broadcasting and on-location reporting made common by the advent of CNN and twenty-four-hour news coverage. It was a prime era to be in the news business.

Eventually, Stewart stopped covering the news in front of the camera and started working behind the scenes to help large companies tell their own stories. Joining his wife, who was then an engineer for telecommunications giant Southwestern Bell, Stewart began his lengthy public-relations career as the company's PR manager in St. Louis. There, he helped coordinate advertising campaigns, became a master of wordplay, and, drawing on his on-camera experience, earned a reputation as a top-notch corporate spokesman.

Soon thereafter, Stewart led public relations activities for Southwestern Bell throughout the United States, Europe, Latin America, and the Caribbean. He later served as American Airlines' chief media spokesman. But American wasn't quite quirky enough for Stewart, he discovered, so he joined Dallas-based rival Southwest Airlines, just in time to help the regional airline grow into one of the nation's busiest and most successful carriers.

First as manager of public relations and ultimately as senior director of the fifteen-person department, Stewart helped Southwest gain recognition as one of the best airlines in the country. One of his crowning achievements was an event in 1992 called "Malice in Dallas," which pitted Southwest founder and chairman Herb Kelleher against the CEO of a small aviation company. The two arm-wrestled for the right to use the slogan "Just Plane Smart," and although Kelleher lost the match, Southwest was allowed to use the slogan. Stewart was once again shown to be a PR guru. Press coverage of the event in outlets ranging from the *Dallas Morning News* to the BBC in London helped spread the company's image as a fun, friendly airline.

Stewart's most difficult task came in the aftermath of the September 11th terrorist attacks. At first, all planes were grounded, then the entire airline industry suffered for months, and many companies eventually approached bankruptcy. Through it all, Stewart's passion for his work helped Southwest hold on—the company was the first to put a plane in the sky after the 9/11 attacks—and remain successful.

But eventually Stewart decided it was time to trade in his free flights around the country for free tickets to just about any concert or entertainment event. He now directs press and marketing activities around the world for Ticketmaster.

Though he doesn't make $7 million a year, which was too little for Latrell Sprewell to feed his family, Stewart assures me that he is living comfortably. Fortunately, he doesn't go home with just a salary—he goes home with a smile on his face because he is doing something he can be passionate about.

Author's note: Since this account was written, Stewart has returned to the airline industry, this time as managing director of external communications for Delta Airlines.

CHAPTER 19

Lynn Tyson

VICE PRESIDENT OF INVESTOR RELATIONS FOR DELL

At the ringing of the bell that closes the stock market each day, Lynn Tyson is focused on an arrow on a computer screen; it points to the stock price of Dell, her employer, and it is pointing either up or down.

Fortunately, Dell has had a lot more ups than downs since Michael Dell started the company nearly twenty-five years ago in his University of Texas dorm room. But when stock analysts and investment experts—people on Wall Street who can influence those ups and downs—think of Dell, they may think of Tyson, the computer giant's vice president for investor relations, known commonly as IR.

In this role, she handles Wall Street matters and relationships for the $55 billion corporation, which ranks among the top forty companies in the United States. Tyson is a widely respected leader in her field. Her experiences and expertise are regularly shared at regional and national conferences and investor events, and she has been profiled by *IR Update*, the National Investor Relations Institute's magazine.

Since Tyson joined the company in 2000, Dell has moved up more than twenty spots on the Fortune 500 list and doubled its revenue, certainly great signs for people on Wall Street. But even with this success, the company has experienced its share of ups and downs in a highly competitive industry. Throughout, Tyson has shared the company's story on Wall Street to improve the company's value and reputation with some of the most important financial decision makers in the world.

In Tyson, Dell has a trusted IR veteran whose department was recognized as one of the nation's best by a top research firm and was recently ranked by *Institutional Investor* magazine as the hardware industry's "most shareholder-friendly company." Tyson has seen her job's profile increase exponentially since Congress created tougher regulations for corporations in the wake of the Enron scandal.

In a 2004 *Treasury and Risk* article titled "If It Walks and Talks Like a CEO, It Could Be IR," Tyson said, "The typical view had always been that investor relations was really just PR [public relations] for investors, and even today a lot of companies still don't realize how important IR can be for them." She added, "A lot of senior executives don't get the role of IR in their own company."

Based at Dell's headquarters, just north of Austin, Texas, Tyson spends her workdays making sure her boss and fellow executives understand what Wall Street is thinking and saying about the company and its competitors. Fittingly, Tyson grew up in New York City, not too far from Wall Street. She was the sole daughter of first-generation Americans who emigrated from the Caribbean. Tyson's parents made sure their daughter and two sons understood the important role of education and learning not only in the classroom, but in everything they did.

"My parents raised us with a keen focus on education and knowing the power of education and its ability to eliminate barriers," said Tyson. "They also made sure that we identified what we loved to do."

Heeding her parent's words of wisdom, Tyson's brothers pursued careers in what they loved. One brother went to the prestigious Rhode Island School of Design and is an accomplished artist, while the other attended Harvard and then graduate school at Columbia to become an astrophysicist.

"Lynn has always been eager to engage in areas of interest to her, and she has a high energy level no matter what she does," said Neil deGrasse Tyson, her astrophysicist brother.

Unfortunately, Tyson wasn't so certain of her career path. For years, she thought her love of horses would lead her to a career as a large-animal veterinarian, but after her sophomore year at Cornell, she started to have second thoughts. Instead of changing majors and hoping for the best, Tyson took a break from school and served as a mounted urban park ranger in New York's Central Park.

Ultimately, she returned to school, at the City College of New York, to pursue a degree in psychology. Her knack for understanding situations and reading people didn't lead her to become a psychologist, but it serves her well in her dealings with the heavy hitters of Wall Street.

While a senior in college, Tyson found herself enjoying both an economics course and an internship at PepsiCo's headquarters in Purchase, New York. Upon graduating, she was offered a full-time job in the company's finance department. Tyson reflected, "I always like to know what's going on, and I realized that in finance I could get a good understanding of the entire company and see what's going on instead of being in a department that was just focused on one thing, like manufacturing."

At PepsiCo, Tyson was further inspired when she noticed one of the company's senior executives was a black man; she envisioned herself following in his footsteps to the executive suite. The company, seeing Tyson as an executive in the making, increased her responsibilities and paid for her to earn a master's degree in finance and international business from New York University's Stern School of Business.

At the time, PepsiCo owned Frito-Lay, Pizza Hut, Taco Bell, and KFC. Tyson moved up the ladder to oversee many of the food division's finance and IR efforts, including a position managing finance in Latin America. After twelve years with

PepsiCo, Tyson left to serve as vice president of IR for a newly formed $20 billion company, now known as Yum! Brands, which combined PepsiCo's three restaurant chains to become the world's largest restaurant operator.

Remembering her tenure at PepsiCo, Tyson said, "I was kind of spoiled at PepsiCo. They were one of the first large companies to have an African American executive, which showed me it was possible to get there, and they did a number of things to help me get more experience and education. The company had a conscience about diversity."

Tyson could not pass on the opportunity to work for Dell, in a young industry that offered plenty of room to grow and learn. When she moved to Texas, she brought her love of horses along with fifteen years of professional experience. She now owns four horses and splits her time away from the office between them and her family.

How does she balance her successful but demanding career with her family, horses included?

"Lynn started at a very entry-level position at Pepsi, but she saw where she wanted to land, and she charted a course to make sure she got there," added her brother Neil. "People are too quick to give up or lose energy to continue, but if you find something you love, you'll have an unlimited supply of energy."

Tyson may not work on Wall Street, but she talks in a quick, straight-to-the-point manner common in New York. When asked what advice she would offer to someone looking to emulate her successful career, she offered three points: "Know what you love to do and what makes you happy. Be your harshest critic. And be unassailable." Do those three things, and your stock can only go up.

CHAPTER 20

Willie Miles, Jr.

FOUNDER AND CEO OF MILES WEALTH MANAGEMENT

Willie Miles, the founder and CEO of Miles Wealth Management, in Houston, manages the financial affairs of fellow business executives, professional athletes, and entertainers. But he remembers a time when the idea of being responsible for vast sums of money was beyond his wildest dreams.

Raised by a single mother, Miles spent his school years in Donaldsonville, Gretna, and New Orleans, Louisiana, where he attended O. P. Walker High School. His mother, a schoolteacher, instilled in him and his sister the importance of education, hard work, and personal integrity.

In high school and on through college, Miles worked as a gas-station attendant. This part-time job fostered an interest in petroleum engineering, and he eventually worked summers for the Shell Oil Company.

After taking courses at both the University of New Orleans and Louisiana State University, Miles worked for Exxon in offshore production, where he made a good living working seven-day shifts. Later, when the rising popularity of computers piqued his curiosity, he secured assignments setting up computer systems at offshore facilities for the drilling department, and for audits in the accounting department.

Ultimately, Miles found himself working exclusively in accounting, which led him back to college to finish his degree, this time at Loyola University. Soon thereafter, Exxon centralized its accounting division and Miles transferred to Houston. Unfortunately, the move led to increased travel and frequent absences from his young family; Miles had to make a choice. Because his daughters were increasingly involved in sports and other extracurricular activities, Miles resigned from Exxon to pursue a career that would allow him more time for himself and his family.

For a few years, Miles pursued entrepreneurial interests, including the marketing of a shoe-care product that he and a friend developed, but never cracked his target market—the military. He eventually decided to go back to work full-time not as an accountant, but as an investment consultant. He had begun his financial training at home, investing his own money in the stock market, which led him to pursue a career in wealth management.

Initially, Miles worked for a major global financial-services firm, which proved to be excellent training. He recalls this as a great way to get into the business and be trained by proven and successful financial managers. Though he wasn't yet making a substantial salary, he understood the importance of paying his dues in order to get the proper training and experience.

Still, Miles had loftier goals than those this position would allow him to achieve. He had a sincere desire to give back directly to the black community that nurtured, molded, and sparked his desire to succeed. He had been given an opportunity to emerge from his humble beginnings, but instead of reaching and seeking for himself, he wanted to reach back and help others by providing opportunities for the less fortunate. His position at that time did not allow for those kinds of philanthropic endeavors.

For seven years, Miles enhanced his knowledge base by working for two successful financial-services firms. While he was at one of these companies, Miles developed an expertise in the area of professional sports, particularly in managing the finances of professional football players. Unfortunately, some of his clients came out of college with poor credit scores because their only money had come from athletic scholarships. The policies of his employer at the time prevented him from issuing checkbooks or debit cards to clients with poor credit scores.

Miles was often placed in the position of telling clients with hundreds of thousands of dollars to their names that he could not issue them the financial tools necessary for wisely managing their financial affairs and improving their credit. Such experiences prompted him to start his own business, run it his way—the right way—and give back to the black community.

After careful planning, Miles walked away from his stable position and steady salary to start Miles Wealth Management. It was a risky move. But the value and quality of his service to his existing clients became evident when more than 95 percent of them put their money in Miles's hands to help Miles Wealth Management hit the ground running. This was a testament to Miles's work ethic, rapport with his clients, and personal integrity. In its first year, his business grow by nearly 50 percent. And now Miles is finally where he wants to be.

Miles said, "It's nice to be able to build the business in the manner that I choose, and support the people and organizations which are important to me." Now, he controls the revenue, he has a personal relationship with each client, and most importantly, he is in a position to give back to the black community directly. He recently brought on a second financial advisor to assist in his growing business, and plans to add more in the near future as the business grows.

Drawing on all that experience in making tough decisions, in his career and his personal life, Miles advises young people to get out of their comfort zone and explore opportunities. He also encourages young black people to be more persistent: "When things are tough or things are not working well, that's when you really learn the most valuable lessons." Considering the wide-ranging career experiences Miles has had and the lessons he has had to learn to become successful, he is someone to listen to.

For those considering a career in financial planning, he warns that it is a business in which you can make a lot of money quickly by doing the wrong thing, but shortcuts don't pay off in the long term. In his line of business, it is easy to be tempted by opportunities to be selfish and think of personal goals first, but ethics requires a focus on doing the right thing.

Miles attributes his success to the importance he has placed on education throughout his life and career. He is always finding ways to learn more and to improve his skills. He credits one of his professors with showing him how to learn from the past, and cited the words of George Santayana: "Those who cannot remember the past are condemned to repeat it."

Miles continues to learn through education and history, but more importantly, he lives by the creed taught to him by his late mother, who reminded him, "Always be honest, and you don't have to explain the truth." The truth for Miles is that choosing personal integrity and honoring his interests over the status quo have made him a true success. Making these tough but smart choices have, like dollars and cents, added up quite nicely for him.

CHAPTER 21

Horace Allen

As a boy, Horace Allen watched helplessly as his father, an unskilled laborer, was repeatedly rejected when he applied to work at General Motors' Fisher Body plant in Syracuse, New York. As a result, Allen's childhood ambition was to become the CEO of General Motors to make sure that hard workers like his father would be treated fairly in the job market.

While Allen didn't become CEO of General Motors, he did become CEO of Total Solutions Group (TSG), a multi-million-dollar company that was based in Minneapolis, Minnesota. After bringing the company back from the verge of bankruptcy, Allen helped Total Solutions Group become a forty-million-dollar technology company in seven years, the largest IBM business partner in Minnesota, and the first minority-owned company to hold a seat on the coveted IBM Americas Business Partner Advisory Council.

Allen's passion for reaching back to help others is demonstrated by his development of TSG University, a nonprofit organization dedicated to teaching technology to underserved communities. After the sale of TSG, Allen founded and became the CEO of TeamPact, a social enterprise whose mission is to work with academic institutions to mentor and facilitate the development of men of color by improving retention, graduation, and employment rates.

Allen was born in Auburn, Alabama. Shortly after his birth, his family moved to the growing industrial area of Syracuse, New York, to improve their standard of living. There they lived in public-housing projects until Allen's junior year in high school. Instead of providing examples of what his life ambitions should be, these experiences taught Allen memorable lessons of what he did not want to do. He constantly fought off the image of poverty while being unwilling to embrace fantasies of wealth. He confessed that much of his success has been driven by the fear of failure. This fear of failure fueled an academic fire that led to his being on the honor roll or dean's list at every level of his education.

With the image of his father's job frustrations permanently etched in his mind, he sought self-employment as a way to be self-sufficient and in control of his own future. Allen admitted he has had only two full-time employers in his life. He worked at McDonald's in high school and for computer maker IBM for eight years after college. For the majority of his professional life, he has been an entrepreneur. Allen said it took him just a year at IBM to realize black wealth is not likely to be created through jobs in corporate America alone, but also through entrepreneurship.

Allen's primary role models were his parents, to whom he attributes his work ethic. Though he admits to buying into the heavily marketed images of sports figures, he attributes much of his success to role models whom he could reach out and touch, such as teachers and coaches. Their influence helped him come up with a phrase that his company has copyrighted: "Education Return on Investment." Horace believes this concept should be taught to today's youth.

Allen exemplified the model student-athlete. He describes the academic setting as an arena where the rules are often crafted to suit the group in power. He likens it to a professional wrestling match, in which the outcome is often determined before the contest begins. Success for minorities in that kind of academic environment requires frequent doses of Allen's strongest advice, similar to Dr. George's: never give up.

Allen thinks that people like him should point young black people in the right direction and give them road maps to success. He believes that today's youth seem to be in survival mode, which to them means watching BET and wearing name-brand icons on their backs. This road map leads nowhere. Allen wants these young people to open their minds and reroute their ideas in order to embrace real success rather than settle for just the symbols of success.

Allen also advises young people to define their goals early and then get the necessary coaching to convert those dreams into reality. He warns that the trial-and-error school of hard knocks is painful and time consuming.

It would be easy for Allen to sit back and enjoy his financial security, boast about his success, and flaunt his many awards. Instead, he remains hard at work, giving back and reaching back to help other achieve and accomplish their dreams.

CHAPTER 22

Deavra Daughtry

PRESIDENT AND CEO OF EXCELLENT CARE MANAGEMENT

Deavra Daughtry recalls spending all day at church on Sunday, then coming home in the evening and watching her grandmother, the church's treasurer, dump the money collected at the services on her bed for counting. She would help her grandmother sort the coins and count the money. Occasionally, imagining she was rich, she would roll around in the money. But she knew that if any of it stuck to her, she had to immediately return it to its proper place or else incur her grandmother's wrath. Daughtry learned an important lesson from this example: it is important to earn people's trust, and continued honesty will keep that trust alive.

Integrity is a characteristic that usually persists throughout adulthood if taught early in life. Daughtry credits the integrity she learned early from her grandmother with helping make her successful today.

Daughtry is president and chief executive officer of Excellent Care Management, one of the nation's largest personal in-home-care agencies. She grew up in the Acres Home community, a low-income area of Houston. It is not a place one would expect to serve as an incubator of CEOs, but Daughtry stands as a testimony to the honesty, integrity, hard work, and faith she learned there. Her love of providing care for those who are unable or less able to care for themselves was inspired by caring for her grandmother. Now her company's more than five hundred employees provide care for a multitude of clients in the Greater Houston area.

Daughtry's immense success did not come immediately; she started out as a volunteer in a State of Texas mailroom. She then was hired as an assistant in the social services department of Harris County, and later worked her way up to social worker, a position she held for eight years. She stumbled across a program that offered services to senior citizens, and realized it was the same kind of assistance—driving them to get prescriptions filled and similar sorts of errands—she was providing for her own grandmother and her grandmother's friends. Once she understood that there was a crucial need for the services she was providing, she recognized the opportunity to start a business.

In 1997, Daughtry's idea became a reality when she completed the licensing process to operate a personal home-assistance services agency; she called hers Excel-E-Care. However, she realized that, as a state employee, she was not eligible to secure state contracts for her small business. She was faced with a choice: expand her business and quit her comfortable state job, with all its benefits and the tenure she had built up over the years, or play it safe and abandon her dream of being of service to people like her "Granny." Deciding not to play in safe, she quit her job "to step out on faith."

It would be nice to say that from that point on everything went fine and she lived happily ever after, but that was not the case. Her ascendance in the business world included two years when she was "totally broke." She spent every penny of her savings, built up from the years she spent in a stable job with the state; at one point she didn't have five dollars to put gas in her car. She warns others who are interested in going into business for themselves that it is not easy to make money initially.

And she couldn't fall back on a financially stable family

for support during the cash-strapped times. Instead, although she lacked a dependable income, she was faced with a house payment, a car payment, electricity and other utility bills, and the need to provide food for her two children. This was a pivotal moment. She had to decide whether to go back and get a nine-to-five job like her old one, or to persevere by remaining focused on her dream of running her own business.

Looking back, Daughtry confesses that she almost had a nervous breakdown, but her seven-year-old daughter came to her, put her arms around her, and uttered some wise-beyond-her-years words that gave Daughtry the encouragement to hold on to her sanity and her dream: "Momma, this is just a test. God is testing you!" Those words gave Daughtry newfound strength and the courage to persist in her quest to make her business successful. From that point, her business began to move forward.

Now, Daughtry credits her success to the quality of care she provides for her clients, but also the support she offers her employees. Because of their high job satisfaction and personal loyalty, employees rarely leave Daughtry's company. And like Daughtry herself, her employees believe in the good work they are doing. Her belief in doing business with integrity, which is reflected throughout her company, is a principle that she credits with the company's success.

Her integrity comes from her desire to serve, and that desire has helped her start a nonprofit group. It began when she counseled a few employees in some basic life skills, and as the response grew, she was prompted to develop in-service sessions for larger numbers of employees. She brought in outside experts to teach checkbook and money management and other essential life skills. As more employees came to the sessions, and began bringing family members to take advantage of the valuable free information, Daughtry decided to start a nonprofit called the Texas Women Empowerment Foundation. This international organization, started in 2003, inspires women to reach their potential.

Daughtry recalls a pivotal moment in the formation of her nonprofit. After noticing similarities between her life and that of Susan Taylor, editor of *Essence* magazine, she asked Taylor to speak at one of her in-service meetings. The usual group of fifty grew to an audience of eight hundred women. Recognizing the magnitude of what had been accomplished, Daughtry went on to establish her foundation and to organize national conferences dedicated to the empowerment of women. Today, her foundation is putting together an international summit featuring business leaders from all over the world.

And even though Daughtry's foundation has gone international, she has not forgotten her roots. She has personally financed the building of the Empowerment Community Center in Houston, which holds free monthly seminars on how to start a business. Daughtry believes in inspiration, so she is providing a vehicle to continually provide it for others. Her collection of awards and accolades prove as much.

She has received a number of honors over the years, including a Certificate of Congressional Recognition, a letter of commendation for community involvement from State Representative Sylvester Turner, an Emerging 10 Award from the Houston Minority Council for innovative business performance, a YMCA Minority Achievers Award for improving the quality of life in Houston, and recognition as one of Houston's top female business owners.

Daughtry drew on her life's challenges and successes to write *Purpose to Blessings: Fourteen Proven Faith Principles for Wealthy Business and Healthy Living,* a book meant to encourage others to find their purpose and pursue their dreams. But despite everything Daughtry has achieved thus far, her most noteworthy accomplishments may still be ahead of her. There is still plenty for her to do both in Houston and abroad. Whatever she achieves, her integrity and willingness to serve and inspire others will always be sources of honor.

Judging from her stewardship of her grandmother, she will be entrusted with the care of others for a long time. At this writing, her seventy-nine-year-old grandmother is still the church treasurer.

CHAPTER 23

Je'Caryous Johnson

FOUNDER AND CEO OF I'M READY PRODUCTIONS

"You don't have to be great to get started, but you have to get started to be great. Period. I don't care what you are doing. Whatever it is that you are choosing to pursue," said Je'Caryous Johnson. With that axiom as his compass, it is no wonder another Houston resident is worthy of being called a real role model. Unlike Rufus Cormier, however, he isn't using his education in court. His jury is an audience.

Johnson, barely more than thirty years old, owns and runs a successful stage-production company called I'm Ready Productions. As his life and career have shown, Johnson has always been ready to get started. He has more than a dozen years of experience in the performing arts, having trained with notable theatre greats including Broadway luminaries and Tony Award winners such as Jose Quintero, Uta Hagen, Edward Albee, Dr. Sidney Berger, and C. Lee Turner. If those names aren't familiar, how about Brian McKnight, Vivica A. Fox, Ginuwine, and Robin Givens? Those are some of the famous actors and multiplatinum singers Johnson has worked with over the years.

Growing up, Johnson looked to his grandparents as role models, and his business savvy likely comes from his grandfather, who was an entrepreneur and owned a landscaping and yard-service company. Johnson noted that his grandfather "wasn't the most educated person, but had a lot of business [sense], but he basically taught me, you know, what it is like to be a hard worker and an entrepreneur. What he showed me was that hard work pays off."

Even as an arts-friendly child growing up in Houston, Johnson never fully envisioned that his hard work would one day lead to a successful career as a playwright career. His work, including _Whatever She Wants_ (starring Vivica Fox), _Men, Money, and Gold Diggers_ (starring R&B singer Ginuwine), and _Cheaters_ (based on the best-selling Eric Jerome Dickey novel and starring Grammy Award winner Brian McKnight), has earned him industry recognition, media attention, and an NAACP Image Award.

Johnson grew up in the same neighborhood that his mother, grandmother, and great-grandmother grew up in. It this lively neighborhood, known as Studewood, Johnson began developing his interest in pleasing audiences, oftentimes putting on small productions for family reunions. He later became interested in producing and writing, and as a freshman in high school, he won a national award for playwriting. He has been racking up accolades and admiration ever since.

After attending historically black Prairie View A&M University, and later the University of Houston, Johnson partnered up with his cousin Gary Guidry, who had been a performer almost as long as Johnson, and started I'm Ready. Guidry, who has played drums, piano, trumpet, and several other instruments since elementary school, would be the musical director, and Johnson would be the production director and playwright.

Once the team was formed, Johnson told the University of Houston's African American Studies Program that he could put on any type of show it needed. This happened to be when the university was gearing up for a Martin Luther King Day celebration. With only a five-hundred-dollar budget, Johnson put on a hit show titled _Slaves to Kings,_ which, Johnson says, "dealt with African Americans from slavery to Martin Luther King." Johnson said, "I stole the event, and so it seemed like overnight I went from a $500 deal to the university asking me to do the next year for $20,000, and that is when I knew that I had found something here, and it was worth investigating and pursuing."

Johnson, at just nineteen, went on to write, direct, produce, and star in *Harlem Renaissance,* which won the first-place medal at the Kennedy Center's National History Competition in 1996. He has performed in more than fifty additional productions, including a performance for President Clinton at the Kennedy Center in 1997. For his talent and hard work, Johnson received the Irene Ryan Award for Excellence in Acting for his portrayal of Lyons in August Wilson's *Fences.*

Winning an award for his work in an August Wilson play isn't the only way Johnson wants to be linked to the legendary Pulitzer- and Tony Award–winning black dramatist. Like Wilson, whose plays chronicle black life from the 1900s to the 1990s, Johnson wants to make productions that "grapple with complex personal, social, and moral themes." Johnson said, "We formed I'm Ready Productions to teach and change people for the good through theater. We wanted to do Shakespeare as well as [August] Wilson. We felt the need to perform diverse works with excellence, to make a statement with our work. We also write and produce educational plays, which we call 'Theater for the Living,' where we teach young adults to deal with social issues like peer pressure, substance abuse, child abuse, rape, and sexually transmitted diseases."

These educational pieces stem from Johnson's understanding of the important role that education has played in his own life and career. He credits his schooling with teaching him the discipline to meet deadlines, stay on budget, and wear the many hats he wears as a business owner and playwright: "You are talking about deadlines and timelines, and meeting those deadlines can affect my bottom line. When you talk about writing projects and producing projects, directing projects, time is always of the essence. I mean, being in school, they kind of teach you a little bit of something about everything. That is why you had to take all these different subjects, and I think that's what life is like. [Education] gave me the discipline and tenacity to go and get it and the fact that if I want it, I can get it."

While Johnson credits God for his success, he says his education taught him to look beyond the classroom and helped him make his dream a reality. Fittingly, Johnson highly recommends a book titled *The Seven Laws of Spiritual Success,* by Deepak Chopra. The book discusses ways to think more effectively in order to increase your success and fulfill your dreams. Based on Johnson's success, it seems he read every word.

But Johnson doesn't need to refer to a book in order to share what he believes to be basic principles for life. First, he said, taking control of life before life takes control of you is essential: "At the end of the day, when the business is all said and done, if you didn't enjoy the journey, it wasn't worthwhile to begin with. So you have to enjoy the journey of it, you know; the end result is what it is. Sometimes it is great, sometimes it is not so great, but the true ordeal is the chase, is the journey."

Second, Johnson understands the importance of charting your own path: "Let's do away with the copycat mentality. If we do that, and you chart your own path, then you can find out your purpose in life. But you can never find out your purpose by trying to live through somebody else's purpose. I would say, it is kind of thinking it until you make it, project it till you perfect it."

And finally, "People say, well, dreams come true or dreams don't come true. I say dreams don't do anything. A dream is the start of something that you must put a plan of action to. So planning—and then a vision."

As a young student, Je'Caryous Johnson may not have had a vision or even an idea of what was in store for him later in life, but he followed his own advice: he got started.

CHAPTER 24

Do We Really Lack Real Role Models?

In 2008, we saw the election of a black man as president of the United States. Many would like to believe that Barack Obama's success answers the question whether the black community has sufficient leadership and powerful enough role models. But such an assumption would be premature.

Many of those profiled here, such as Leonard Pitts and Tracie Hall, may be too young to remember every detail of the civil rights era—just as President Obama is—but they fully understand that they wouldn't be where they are today without the contributions made during that time. During the civil rights movement, there seemed to be an abundance of blacks to admire, and emulate. Today young blacks are encouraged to admire and emulate and idolize only blacks who appear on TV, play professional sports, star in movies, and perform rap songs.

This is not to say that black athletes and entertainers have not been inspiring throughout U.S. history; after all, we have been greatly uplifted by musicians like Quincy Jones, who helped make Michael Jackson a superstar, and Aretha Franklin, the queen of soul, as well as by sports figures like Jackie Robinson and Olympic great Jackie Joyner-Kersey, but some things have changed. If you look closely enough, it is hard to believe they have changed for the better when it comes to identifying black role models.

Oddly enough, things got started on this course during the civil rights movement when several black celebrities made their voices heard. Entertainer Harry Belafonte, gospel singer Mavis Staples, and the young poet Maya Angelou all raised their profiles greatly during the late sixties and early seventies.

Even today, Angelou, along with others like Jesse Jackson, publicly discuss problems affecting blacks. And while their voices are powerful and their causes great, the fact that the black community still relies heavily on these people, who shined mostly in the years right after Dr. King's passing, proves the present need for new role models and leaders to connect with younger blacks, who identify more with Sean "P. Diddy" Combs and Kobe Bryant than Stokely Carmichael and Jackie Robinson.

Dozens of historians and activists have pointed to the decline in black leadership since the assassinations of Malcolm X and Dr. King.

Unfortunately, to fill this void, black children have often tried to find the next-best examples of professional success and social advancement. Since the 1970s, the best examples, it seems, have been entertainers, whether in comedy, music, or sports. Today, we commonly look to these celebrities in these fields to serve as the main role models and leaders in the black community. Here are a few black celebrities who became role models outside of civic causes or churches.

Before he was Muhammad Ali, Cassius Clay was a Kentucky-born boxer who won nearly every amateur boxing award on his way to winning the gold medal as a light heavyweight in the 1960 Olympics. Eventually, he became a three-time world heavyweight champion and one of the greatest sports figures of all time. Out of the ring, however, Ali was less in command, being known for loose friendships, bad finances, and womanizing. *Sports Illustrated* named him "Sportsman of the Century" in 1999, ahead of Michael Jordan, Babe Ruth, and Jim Brown, whom many consider the best football player of all time.

By the time Jim Brown retired, in 1965, the Georgia native had become the most prolific running back in professional football history, earning three MVP awards and setting countless records while playing with the Cleveland Browns. Like Ali, Brown used his fame to speak out on social issues and help the civil rights and black empowerment movements. However, Brown also was known as a misogynist and, more than once, failed to treat women with respect, something that later became common in rap music.

Before there was rap music, there was James Brown (no relation to Jim Brown). Known by a slew of titles, most notably the "Godfather of Soul" and the "Hardest Working Man in Show Business," Brown became prominent in the late fifties, but used his fame to support the civil rights cause in the sixties. Having grown up in South Carolina and Georgia, Brown was familiar with racism and segregation. His 1968 hit song "Say It Loud—I'm Black and I'm Proud" helped Brown become a leader at a time when many young blacks were becoming unsupportive of more traditional civil rights leaders, Dr. King included.

While Ali, Jim Brown, and James Brown were key voices during those years, they also had personality flaws that later led historians and others to downplay or question their roles as black leaders since the civil rights movement. Perhaps without acknowledging it at the time, the black community embraced them as activists not because of what they truly believed in, but because of what they were able to do professionally. This trend has continued with athletes, entertainers, and rappers today.

However, admiring these men for their professional success was not a mistake. Nor was it a mistake to take heed of the causes they promoted. However, their paths to activism created a trend within the black community in which we identify with black celebrities before we learn about the issues. In other words, since the civil rights movement, we have become accustomed to promoting celebrities more than their causes.

Today, thanks to the foundation laid by those men, we routinely look to celebrities like Michael Jordan, Chris Rock, and Will Smith—rather than politicians and people who determine policy—to speak out on social and political issues confronting the black community. Oftentimes, white presidential candidates seek the endorsement of black celebrities instead of looking to blacks who have spent decades in public service.

So although the civil rights movement's leaders were not perfect people by any means, the acceptance of Ali and James Brown, in particular, as their replacements or equals had the adverse effect of lowering our expectations for our leaders and role models. Over the years, our concept of black role models has narrowed as professional sports has become a multi-billion-dollar enterprise and entertainment, from music to comedy, has grown in scope and influence around the world.

Today, comedian Richard Pryor is better known than Richard Parsons, the chairman of Citigroup. More black boys grow up idolizing Olympic gold medalist and runner Michael Johnson than author and professor Michael Eric Dyson. And Whitney Houston is more easily identified by young black girls than Sheila Jackson-Lee, a congresswoman from Houston, Texas.

It is not unusual to see even young white kids admiring and emulating black athletes and rappers rather than their white counterparts. This is an accomplishment for blacks in America, but it does not speak to the gap between the types of professional avenues available to whites—namely, the ability to attend prestigious universities and make higher incomes—and those offered to their black peers.

Within the black community, there is a clear overemphasis on black celebrities as role models. Black children and teens spend countless hours playing sports, yet very few make it to college because of their athletic ability. Similarly, football star Michael Vick was held up as more likely to be a role model for black boys than Condoleezza Rice, the former secretary of state. Why is this so uncomfortably close to truth?

In a 2007 article titled "Culture and Race Affect Job Opportunities," Furrah Qureshi, then a student at Drexel University, wrote: "Perpetuating the notion that an entire race of people should occupy one select field is ridiculous as well as detrimental because the chances for success are less likely, meaning failure is more likely, meaning, the culture is setting them up to fail."

One of the ways we set our young black people up to fail is by limiting the scope of possible role models. Qureshi adds, "Today, there is a notion that the only way for an African American to be successful is to become either a rapper or a sports star." In other words, if you are a successful black person, it is probably because you are a celebrity or you work with them; it has very little to do with getting an education.

If the goals and aspirations of young blacks remain focused on sports and entertainment, the next generation is likely to fail to build on the foundation laid by Dr. King and his successors. How do we know? Numbers don't lie. Millions of black children are investing their energy, hopes, and dreams on two very narrowly focused fields that are extremely difficult to enter.

For example, in the realm of sports, sociologist Jay Coakley conservatively estimates that there were about 6,000 people making a living as professional athletes in 2008. Even if all of those positions were filled by black players, there would be more opportunity in dozens of other professional fields. Recent studies tallied more than 40,000 black doctors, nearly 50,000 black lawyers, and at least 100,000 black engineers, to name only a few professional careers that are far more accessible than professional sports. And some of those doctors, lawyers, and engineers almost surely played high school or even college sports.

What is even more surprising is that, according to salary studies, people in these professions will have higher lifetime earnings than the average professional athlete. But this book isn't about doing finding job that pays the most or is the easiest to get into. Instead, we are identifying other ways to become a success, and a role model, without betting everything one throw of the dice.

Qureshi, the student quoted earlier, went on to write, "With these disproportional statistics, the task seems so much more difficult. We're not just combating an economic issue; we have to combat a cultural issue." While not every doctor or lawyer is a role model, neither is every NBA or NFL player, and black doctors, lawyers, and engineers outnumber professional athletes nearly thirty to one, so there is a good chance of finding a role model at a local hospital or courtroom.

As Qureshi pointed out, there is a cultural hurdle to overcome. We should rethink why the black community as a whole has been somewhat reluctant to encourage young blacks to identify with role models like a high school principal or a local city council member.

Black kids spend thousands of hours every year on football fields and basketball courts and singing in youth choirs, but where are the programs that encourage them to practice becoming doctors, lawyers, and educators? There is nothing wrong with playing sports and trying to get a college scholarship through sports, but many black youths, it seems, are unaware of their actual chances of making it to the professional ranks. Perhaps they are misled by the number of blacks in the NBA, WNBA, and NFL (not to mention the *Billboard* charts or MTV countdowns).

I played sports throughout my life and coached for several years, and Joah ran track throughout high school and still runs competitively, so obviously we are not against people being interested in sports. But the reality behind professional sports reinforces the low probability of finding success as an adult if young black people fail to make education a top priority.

The National Collegiate Athletic Association (NCAA) puts out a chart that shows the odds a high school athlete becoming a

TABLE: HIGH SCHOOL AND COLLEGIATE STUDENT-ATHLETES REACHING THE PROFESSIONAL LEAGUES
(A COMPARISON ACROSS SIX SPORTS)

	Number of student-athletes					
	Men's basketball	Women's basketball	Football	Baseball	Men's ice hockey	Men's soccer
High school students	546,335	452,929	1,071,775	470,671	36,263	358,935
HS seniors	156,096	129,408	306,221	134,477	10,361	102,553
Students in college (NCAA) programs	16,571	15,096	61,252	28,767	3,973	19,793
College freshman roster positions	4,735	4,313	17,501	8,219	1,135	5,655
HS seniors moving on to college programs (%)	3.0	3.3	5.7	6.1	11.0	5.5
College senior roster positions	3,682	3,355	13,612	6,393	883	4,398
College athletes drafted by the pros	44	32	250	600	33	76
College seniors moving on to the pros (%)	1.2	1.0	1.8	9.4	3.7	1.7
HS seniors moving on to the pros (%)	0.03	0.02	0.08	0.45	0.32	0.07

Note: Percentages are based on estimated data and should be considered approximations. *Source:* http://www.ncaa.org.

college athlete, and then becoming a professional athlete. This chart reveals that most black youths are, in essence, playing the lottery to get into professional sports. Fewer than one in two thousand makes it from high school basketball to the pros, and fewer than one in a thousand makes it from high school football to the NFL.

Regardless of statistics, young people should be encouraged to go after their goals with commitment and hard work. But if they choose sports, they should go after that dream with education front and center. Even with a skilled crossover dribble or a great throwing arm, an education is the foundation of lifetime success.

Look at Shaquille O'Neal, one of the wealthiest and most successful basketball players ever. Even while picking up an MVP trophy and four championship rings, he has stayed focused on the goal of becoming a police officer. He not only made sure he went back to college and earned his degree, after having left early for the NBA, but he also worked with police departments in California and Florida to get trained as an officer. In addition, he picked up a master's degree in business administration, and has said he wants to get a doctorate in criminal justice.

If one of the richest men in sports has a backup plan that involves getting a good education, so should all of us.

CHAPTER 25

Steve Jones

COFOUNDER OF A GRAPHIC DESIGN COMPANY

Democracy. Superpower. Free speech. Freedom of religion. Land
of opportunity. These are a few of the words and phrases that
come to mind when we think of how the United States is per-
ceived around the world. Steve Jones, a graphic designer and
lifelong student of culture and imagery, believes it is a mistake
to think that any of those things are what most makes America
significant. "I know a lot of people think about democracy and
our military and those types of things as America's greatest influence in the world," said Jones. "In reality, America's greatest influence may be this idea of popular culture." Pop culture—consisting of concepts, images, and stereotypes—and
its importance in American and world culture are key determi-
nants of what we experience each day, according to Jones.

In fifteen-plus years in graphic design, Jones has used his
keen understanding of American pop culture and the images
behind its history to break down misperceptions and stereotypes while creating empowering and engaging images. Like
Jones, his output is impressive. Groups that have commis-
sioned design work from him include the African American
Wellness Project, an organization that promotes health and
access to health care; the Vagabond Poet's Café, a Washington,
D.C.–based spoken-word series; and Communities of Opportunity, an effort by the City of San Francisco and local philan-
thropists to improve underprivileged neighborhoods.

It is no surprise Jones has a knack for supporting nonprofit and community-based organizations with his skills. He views much of his work as a public service, since he helps his clients, through his design company plantain, understand the power of images to carry a message. According to the website for plantain: "We seek a unique balance between design and life, form and function, the individual and the collective," and the studio's work is described as "a fusion of culture, politics and ideas, intended to help fill the cultural void within the current design landscape."

Although Jones sees a void in the current landscape, he is also very inspired by it. After attending the California College of the Arts (CCA), where he later taught, Jones received his master's in graphic design from the prestigious Rhode Island School of Design (RISD). His thesis was a mock-up of a magazine called *Black,* which looked at the use of black icons and roles, many established before and during slavery, in the mass media to create such famous marketing figures as Aunt Jemima and Uncle Ben. "[Steve] is a young, talented designer whose unique style draws on diverse and eclectic cultural influences. Perhaps what best defines Steve's practice, however, in my mind at least, is his thoughtful relationship toward content," said Maria Emmighausen, a former colleague. "His interests focus on black icons and their representation in mass media and popular culture, identity politics, and public art."

Jones's thesis research on those icons uncovered a sad reality: blacks continue to be depicted in positions of ignorance and inferiority through the use of images made common before and during the Jim Crow era, when blacks were routinely segregated and degraded. The cover of *Vogue* in April 2008, featuring LeBron James, drew criticism for its offensive imagery. (The photo showed a roaring, teeth-baring James with his arm around smiling Gisele Bundchen; many thought the image was a reference to King Kong holding a white woman.) To offset these negative images, Jones created mock advertisements that showed similar people and identical products from a less stereotypical or prejudicial viewpoint.

Jones's viewpoint is that not only of a black man, but also of a nonnative American: he was born in Canada and spent many of his childhood years in Jamaica. His father, a financial planner, and mother, a schoolteacher, moved to California's Bay Area when political turmoil increased in Jamaica during the late 1970s. Still, Jones is drawn to his ancestral home. "I'm inspired by Jamaica because it's a Third World country," said Jones, who returns to the island nation every couple of years. "In Third World countries, they don't have things like in America and developed nations, so you have to be more resourceful and everything is reused and multipurpose."

Along with being motivated by the concept of turning a jelly jar into a drinking glass, Jones is intrigued by word-heavy art and design, such as Spike Lee films. As a young man, he was fascinated by type and photography, which eventually led to his decision to study design in college. "College is really the first place you're in an environment where you have teachers that have taught design," said Jones. "Design is a way to respond to questions about the world and society and culture."

Given the small number of minorities working in graphic design, it is easy to understand why Jones's master's thesis represented such a critical juncture in his professional career. Seeing himself as a black graphic designer, Jones often seeks out opportunities to bring young blacks into the field. By increasing the diversity of his profession, Jones believes pop culture will be moved closer to mirroring society and all its citizens, both in America and around the world. With that in mind, Jones lectures at San Francisco State University and the CCA about the role of graphic design as a medium that can make either a positive or negative impact. He encourages his students to be responsible with their work and to understand its power. "I see my role as a global citizen, because when you're creating something, you have a certain power," said

Jones, who has also done work for BET and *YSB* magazine. "I honestly believe that it should be a requirement for anyone with talents to teach and share their thoughts and experiences with young people."

Not surprisingly, Jones was a mentor to minority students while at RISD, and now regularly spends time with young artists to help foster their talents and open their eyes to the power of imagery. And Jones should have their full attention. His work is prominently featured all around the Bay Area, everywhere from the Yerba Buena Center for the Arts, where he created a Black Panther–inspired piece, to downtown Oakland's I-880 underpass. His projects "Movemeant: Migrations & Matters" and "Urban Legends: The City in Maps" have both been displayed at the Oaklandish Gallery; he has also shown at the San Francisco African-American Historical and Cultural Society and the Urban League of Rhode Island.

Drawn from America's history and displayed from coast to coast, Jones's images are yet another way to help improve how Americans see their past and future. Because if popular culture makes this nation's greatest impact on the world, Jones wants to help shape it.

CHAPTER 26

Isiah Warner, PhD

PROFESSOR OF CHEMISTRY AT LOUISIANA STATE UNIVERSITY

Nobel Prize–winning chemist Sir Cyril Norman Hinshelwood once called science "an imaginative adventure of the mind seeking truth in a world of mystery." According to Isiah Warner, that would mean he has been a scientist for almost his entire life. "I was destined to be a scientist because I did my first chemistry experiment at the age of two," said Warner, who is the Philip W. West Professor of Analytical and Environmental Chemistry at Louisiana State University.

While still a toddler in the small town of Bunkie, Louisiana, Warner noticed that his parents would put out a mysterious lamp, which required no electricity, but was instead powered by a strange liquid and a small wick. One day when his parents forgot to lock up the strange liquid, the inquisitive youngster took it upon himself to taste the substance to find out for himself exactly how the lamp held the light. The well-respected chemistry professor's first experiment wasn't exactly a success. "They rushed me thirty miles away to the nearest hospital, and from what I am told, I had tubes up my nose and every orifice to try to get the kerosene out of me!"

After a ten-year hiatus from experimenting, Warner was again seized by curiosity, and he proceeded to succeed in every science and math course he took. Oddly enough, although none of Warner's parents or immediate family members made it past ninth grade (his father later received a GED), performing well in school came fairly naturally for him. And even though his family members lacked high school or college educations, Warner said, "My grandmother was a very prominent figure in my life and had a big impact on me. And I often tell people that they [grandmother and parents] motivated [me] to go on and get an education." And that is exactly what Warner did.

"I hated missing school. I averaged [maybe] one absence a year. I just didn't miss school, because I loved school." Warner attended segregated schools, and school would often let out early to allow students to work in the hot cotton fields. "I said, I have no idea what I am going to do but it is not going to be [picking cotton]." That was around the same time his grandmother encouraged him to pursue a career in teaching.

Along with his grandmother, Warner's other major influences, namely, his priest and his music teacher, were helping him realize his potential. He recalls working hard to be the best altar boy in order to win a silver dollar after church. Warner, it seems, just wanted to know he had it in him.

On a recent return trip to his old music teacher's classroom to "tell him what an inspiration he was to me," Warner said, "I was doing what I thought was my best, but he would push me to do things that I didn't even realize I was capable of. And I suddenly realized that my vision of my best was not the same as his vision of my best, and he'd always push me to a higher level that I didn't even think about. The last time I visited, I was talking to him and he had tears in his eyes. I guess he didn't realize what kind of impact he had on me," Warner added.

Warner eventually graduated as valedictorian of his high school and earned a scholarship to Southern University in Baton Rouge. When his high school English teacher found out that he planned to study science, the teacher put him in touch with the chair of Southern's chemistry department. That was when he found out about a summer program that cost $120;

the professor offered to pay half if Warner covered the rest. After convincing his father to give him the $60, Warner found himself in a program with other talented black students who shared his interest in chemistry. By the end of that summer, the professor made a deal with Warner that allowed him to skip first-year chemistry if he made the field his major. Ever since, Warner has been a chemist.

It was that same chemistry department chair who introduced Warner to the concept of adding the title "Dr." in front of his name. "He told me, 'Mr. Warner you will have a PhD before you are thirty.' I said 'Why? What is a PhD?' I had no idea what a PhD was. I thought we called him doctor because he had some kind of medical degree. How can you aspire for a PhD if you don't know what it is!?"

Well, Warner's lack of information didn't stop him from heeding his professor's words. After graduating from Southern, Warner moved to Seattle, Washington, where he earned a doctorate in analytical chemistry from the University of Washington.

Returning to the South, Warner rose quickly from assistant professor at Texas A&M University to associate professor and later full professor at Emory University. He then moved back to his home state to accept his current professorship at LSU. Throughout, Warner has sat on chemistry and science boards and participated in numerous research projects.

Warner has secured millions of dollars in education and research grants for LSU's science-based programs, and has written more than two hundred articles and given hundreds of speeches on his findings and expertise. He has also helped three dozen chemistry students secure their own PhDs by chairing their dissertation committees; many of them have gone on to careers as professors at other universities or as chemists for leading research companies. Just like his professor before him, he makes a point of passing the torch to future black science professionals.

Over the years, Warner has rightfully picked up his share of accolades, including a 1984 Presidential Young Investigator Award, the Most Outstanding Graduate from the Southern University Department of Chemistry, an American Association for the Advancement of Science Fellow, and Tuskegee University's George Washington Carver Achievement Award. It is safe to say that he is one of the foremost chemistry educators in the nation.

Along with being the West Professor of Analytical and Environmental Chemistry (since 1992), Warner is also the owner of two elite professorial titles. He is a Boyd Professor, which is the highest honor bestowed on a professor in the Louisiana State University System. Colleagues and friends wrote more than one hundred letters in support of his garnering this prestigious title. Also, he is a Howard Hughes Medical Institute Professor, an honor bestowed on only twenty professors in the country when the program began, in 2002.

Aside from his status as one of the nation's leading chemistry educators and one of the highest-regarded professors in Louisiana, Warner is also LSU's vice chancellor for strategic initiatives. This job entails working closely with undergraduates and administrators to improve the mentoring of students, faculty, and staff in order to maximize the university's overall success. He has also been active in selecting university leaders, including the school's president and the system's chancellor.

Likewise, his is charged with creating a campus environment in which all students (particularly black students) can excel in science, technology, engineering, and math courses. It is no surprise LSU's graduate program in chemistry is the nation's largest producer of black PhDs in chemistry.

At a time when everyone from members of Congress to Tiger Woods laments the poor state of science and math education in this country, Warner perfectly embodies why minority students should be encouraged to follow their curiosity and imagination into a career in science. Warner added, "Technology is advancing at such a rapid rate that now the college degree is equivalent to what a high school diploma was in my day and age. So you have to go beyond that college degree to get more education, because education is the secret to it all. In the future, education is the one thing that is going to make a difference, and nobody can take education and knowledge from you once you get it."

Warner feels an obligation to mentor young black students because of the people who put things in perspective for him and showed him the way to reaching his potential. In this way, he is paving the way for more scientists, and perhaps more answers to our current problems will follow.

CHAPTER 27

Gloria Ladson-Billings, PhD

PROFESSOR OF EDUCATION AT THE
UNIVERSITY OF WISCONSIN

Gloria Ladson-Billings knows a thing or two about the importance of education. She is the Kellner Family Professor in Urban Education and an H. I. Romnes fellow in the Department of Curriculum and Instruction at the University of Wisconsin–Madison. Somehow, even with all of that, her title doesn't nearly capture Ladson-Billings's life's work.

Over the years, she has established quite a reputation as an educator, author, and critical race theorist in the field of education. Her books *Crossing over to Canaan: The Journey of New Teachers in Diverse Classrooms* and *The Dreamkeepers: Successful Teachers of African American Children* are classics in the area of multicultural education and required reading for many of those preparing to become teachers or seeking advanced degrees in education.

As a child growing up in West Philadelphia, Ladson-Billings had relatively modest goals; at one point, she and her brother aspired only to make a hundred dollars a week and be able to purchase their own television sets. As a professional, she is now one of the most sought-after speakers in higher education; her brother, who obtained an master's in business administration from the prestigious Wharton School at the University of Pennsylvania, has recently retired from a long and rewarding career at IBM.

Ladson-Billings recalls that a significant point in her educational experience came when her mother decided not to send her to the neighborhood middle school and instead enrolled her in a school across town that would challenge her and further her abilities in the classroom.

That was Ladson-Billings's first experience of attending school as a minority, racially and socioeconomically. Growing up in West Philadelphia, most of the neighborhood schools were predominantly black; her new school was predominantly white. This experience, along with a college career that began just before the assassination of Malcolm X and ended just after the assassination of Dr. Martin Luther King, had a memorable impact on her life and her decision to pursue a career in education.

Similarly, Ladson-Billings was profoundly affected by her fifth-grade teacher, who, she said, affirmed early on the brilliance that is now evident to those who read her books and hear her speak. She was also inspired by her father, a laborer with only a fourth-grade education. She stated that even though he was not formally educated, he was the wisest person she knew. She recalled one of her father's wise sayings: "If you see a good fight, get in it." Ladson-Billings has enthusiastically engaged in the fight to improve education of and for children of color throughout her career.

Still, upon entering college, Ladson-Billings was not immediately attracted to teaching. Stirred by the deaths of two of the most prominent and influential leaders in black society, as well as by the climate precipitated by the Vietnam War, Ladson-Billings was moved to do something that would "change society." Ultimately, she realized teaching was one way to do just that.

Ladson-Billings cites another defining moment in her career. As a science and social studies consultant in the Philadelphia school system, she became a victim of budget cuts and had to return to classroom teaching. Though happy to return to teaching, she was informed by a colleague that the only difference between her and the consultants who retained their positions was that they had doctorate degrees.

Motivated to advance in her field, and hoping to escape the Philadelphia winters, she began looking into graduate programs in urban education. After considering several offers, she decided to attend Stanford University, one of the top schools in the country. She believes attending Stanford and its highly rated College of Education made people listen more closely to her advice and provided her with opportunities that may not have been available otherwise. Even after graduating from Stanford, she did not envision a career as a professor. Her goals were still modest: return to Philadelphia and possibly lead the curriculum department in the public school system she once consulted for.

Instead, Ladson-Billings has risen to become one of the nation's top experts on preparing culturally competent teachers (teachers equipped for multicultural student settings) and developing teaching practices to improve the education of children of color. And Ladson-Billings still has many concerns about the education of young black students. Unlike those who condemn youth for their behavior and personal choices, she believes that young people are making the best choices with the information available to them. She wonders whether we can "give them better information, so that they can make better choices, and can we make it less difficult for them?" She is concerned that the demands on our youth are greater than in previous generations and that their futures are much less certain. Thankfully, she is still hard at work to address these issues, for students of color in particular.

Her strong appetite for reading, her love for learning, and a sincere commitment to the public good have contributed to Ladson-Billings's sterling success. She believes those attributes characterize who she is as a person and would be present regardless of her career choice. Her advice to young people aspiring to follow in her footsteps is to focus their aspirations on a "life's work." "If that life's work is facilitated by being a professor, then do that," she said. She advises her graduate students not to look for a job, but figure out what their "work" is, then find a job that will allow them to do their work.

Her accomplishments attest to the fact that Ladson-Billings has certainly found her own life's work. She received the Palmer O. Johnson outstanding research award in 1995, and was awarded an Honorary Doctorate, from Umeå University, in Sweden. She also received the George and Louise Spindler Award from the Council on Anthropology and Education in 2004. Ladson-Billings was elected to membership in the National Academy of Education, and she is a senior fellow in urban education of the Annenberg Institute for School Reform at Brown University.

Ladson-Billings is the author of numerous journal articles and book chapters, and several books on education. Also, she recently served as president of the American Educational Research Association and gave a presidential address that burned the ears of the overflowing crowd in San Francisco. Her address was titled "From the Achievement Gap to the Education Debt: Understanding Achievement in U.S. Schools," and the normally docile group of educators were pierced by her poignant words and acknowledged her brilliance with a thunderous and extended round of applause.

Though her accomplishments are many and outstanding, Ladson-Billings maintains a humble demeanor and down-to-earth spirit. She defers to the Bible for her favorite words of inspiration, which describe the acute necessity of the important work she engages in: "And who knoweth whether thou art come to the kingdom for such a time as this?" (Esther 4:14).

Professor Gloria Ladson-Billings may not have a kingdom of her own, but she has certainly reached the mountaintop of her life's work.

CHAPTER 28

Bernard Muir and Craig Littlepage

ATHLETIC DIRECTOR OF GEORGETOWN UNIVERSITY;
ATHLETIC DIRECTOR OF THE UNIVERSITY OF VIRGINIA

Not all real role models today look to the civil rights movement for their own models of success. Many look to sports for inspiration.

In a report titled "Upward Mobility through Sport?" D. Stanley Eitzen cites a survey conducted by the Center for the Study of Sport in Society, which showed that "two-thirds of African American males between the ages of 13 and 18 believe that they can earn a living playing professional sports (more than double the proportion of young white males who hold such beliefs)." So although there are a great number of black males in professional sports, there are a far greater number of young black students who believe they will become one of them. While blacks are overrepresented among the athletes on basketball courts and football fields, they are less often seen in the coaching ranks or in the offices of athletic departments.

Bernard Muir, athletic director for Georgetown University, is a prime example of how blacks can make a living in sports without ever having to strap on a helmet or lace up a pair of Air Jordans. In fact, two men whose preferred path is sports, Muir and his own role model of sorts, Craig Littlepage, of the University of Virginia, are both worthy of emulation.

Along with the University of Southern California's Mike Garrett, Ohio State University's Gene Smith, and the University of Georgia's Damon Evans, Littlepage and Muir are among the growing number of black athletic directors at major universities. They are also friends, despite a seventeen-year age difference, and colleagues. They chat regularly about their careers, their departments, and their successes. But the two men also share some lessons from the past. It is how they learned those lessons that makes each unique.

Littlepage grew up in a Philadelphia suburb, where his father was a longtime government employee and his mother was a bank teller for many years. In this working-class household, Littlepage learned the importance of bringing a strong work ethic to everything he did. One part of this work ethic, according to Littlepage, is the importance of "showing up." It seems simple enough: a job cannot be done if you are not there, on time, to complete it. For example, when his older brother grew tired of his paper route, Littlepage quickly proved himself a capable paperboy. He credits this first job with teaching him the significant role customer service plays in any job.

Muir, the only child of a real estate agent and a nurse, learned some of the important skills needed to be an athletic director in a slightly different way. Muir was raised in Gainesville, Florida, home of the University of Florida, and it was there, in the backyard of one of the nation's best athletic programs, that he discovered his desire to be around college sports. As a teen, Muir put himself in a position to learn from the sports administrators, coaches, and other athletic staffers—anyone from the strength and conditioning coach to the ticket salesman. There wasn't a job Muir wasn't willing to do; at one point he sold sodas and orange juice at Florida Gators football games. As any athletic director will tell you, fund-raising, game operations, coaching, and marketing are all just parts of the big puzzle of overseeing major-college sports programs. Muir, by exposing himself to a top-rated athletic department, learned that from an early age.

While both Littlepage and Muir spent their high school years on the basketball court, it was their work in the classroom that really set them apart. Thanks to their academic aptitude and effort, both were admitted to Ivy League universities—Littlepage to the University of Pennsylvania, and Muir to Brown University. Although the two young men followed different paths during their college days, each became the first college graduate in his immediate family.

Littlepage helped his Penn basketball team to three Ivy League championships and NCAA tournament appearances, but didn't become interested in sports administration until he had a chat with a friend who had recently accepted a job as a head coach at a nearby university.

Following graduation, Littlepage backed into a job as an assistant basketball coach at Villanova University. After another assistant-coaching job, at Yale, Littlepage began what would be his first of two stints at the University of Virginia. From 1976 to 1982, he was an assistant coach for a budding basketball program that would eventually recruit the nation's top player in the early 1980s, Ralph Sampson.

With the success of the Sampson years, Littlepage was starting to garner more attention in coaching and administrative circles. Eventually, his alma mater came calling. As head coach at Penn, Littlepage said he was humbled by the role. Although he had spent several years as a player and an assistant, he realized he needed to take a "good step back, to humble myself" in order to move forward and find success.

After another head-coaching job, at Rutgers University from 1985 to 1988, Littlepage returned to the University of Virginia, where he began eyeing the more substantial role of administrator. In 1990, he went from assistant coach to assistant athletic director, and later to associate and senior associate athletic director; each job brought increased responsibilities. At one point, in 1994, Littlepage was named interim athletic director before a permanent replacement was named.

After proving himself in challenging roles in the department, Littlepage became the first African American athletic director in Atlantic Coast Conference history. Since taking over in 2001, he has shepherded Virginia to multiple ACC and national titles, and his success has led to his being named one of the most powerful sports figures in the country by *Sports Illustrated* and *Black Enterprise*.

Unlike Littlepage, Muir never fancied himself the coaching type. He always envisioned being in a leadership role off the court. As a freshman, he approached the Brown athletic director in hopes of gaining administrative experience. Muir lettered for four years on the basketball court and studied organizational behavior and management in the classroom.

After earning his degree, he quickly set forth on a successful career as an athletics administrator, accepting various roles with Brown, Butler University, and Ohio University, and later with the NFL's Atlanta Falcons, to learn the tricks of the trade.

After brief stints at Auburn University and Streetball Partners International, a sports marketing firm, Muir began an eight-year job with the NCAA. He started as assistant director of the Men's Division I Basketball Championship, commonly referred to as "March Madness," before being promoted to director. As director of the tournament, Muir ran one of the most popular and highly viewed annual sporting events in the nation.

Before joining Georgetown, Muir gained valuable experience at another prestigious university, Notre Dame. As senior associate athletic director for student welfare and development, he worked to ensure that each student-athlete tried to be as good in the classroom as he or she was on the court. Later, as deputy director of athletics, he managed game operations, athletics facilities, and intramural sports.

In 2005, Muir was named director of athletics for Georgetown, which is best known for its successful basketball program. Coached by the legendary John Thompson and led on the court by all-American Patrick Ewing, who went on to become an NBA Hall of Famer, Georgetown won the 1985 NCAA title. Over the years, several other NBA players have come out of the prestigious university including Dikembe Mutumbo, Alonzo Mourning, and Allen Iverson.

Now, with Thompson's son, John III, keeping the Hoyas basketball squad in national contention, it is Muir's job to continue the winning tradition while ensuring every other sports team at the university achieves the same high level of success.

Championships aside, Muir appears to be following Littlepage's footsteps in another positive way: he is holding the door open for others to follow his path to success. For that, both Littlepage and Muir have become all-star-caliber role models without ever having "gone pro."

Author's note: Muir has since left Georgetown to become athletic director at the University of Delaware.

CHAPTER 29

Beverly Kearney

WOMEN'S TRACK COACH AT THE UNIVERSITY
OF TEXAS AT AUSTIN

Resilience! The *New Oxford American Dictionary* defines *resilient* as "able to withstand or recover quickly from difficult conditions." We suggest Oxford replace the definition with the name "Beverly Kearney."

"Bev," as she is called by her friends, is the ultimate depiction of resilience. Although she is currently the head women's track coach at the University of Texas, her life began in less enviable circumstances. She was born in Mississippi, the sixth of seven children, and grew up also in Florida, California, and Nebraska. She vividly remembers watching her grandmother in Mississippi cook on a wood-burning stove and heat water for bathing. There was no indoor plumbing, so she had to use an outhouse.

As a child, she witnessed alcohol abuse, sexual abuse, and violence. Her brother was the victim of a drive-by shooting as he sat on the front porch of their California home. Because their mother suffered from alcohol addiction, Kearney and her younger brother learned independence at an early age. She vividly remembers as a fifth grader traveling with only her younger brother by bus from Nebraska to California and back.

Kearney painfully recalls that her mother drank for most of her life. She knew her father, but he was in and out of her life, and her mother raised the family on her own. Tragically,

Kearney's mother died of a stroke during her senior year in high school.

Though she was not pushed to excel in school, her competitive nature drove her to maintain an A and B average. School, for Kearney, was a sanctuary. Though she loved her mother and family, she viewed school as a haven. "Everyone else couldn't wait to go home, but I couldn't wait to go to school," she reflected. School was a place where she could be someone else and somewhere else. Though she doesn't classify herself as nerdy or even especially studious, she did find school to be an escape from an otherwise less-than-ideal home life.

Kearney also benefited from an outspoken personality that contributed to her popularity as a student. However, her popularity couldn't erase her racial identity. Kearney remembered a particularly painful racial incident: she won the election for class president at a predominantly white school, "but the vote was close, so they kept recounting the votes." On about the third or fourth recount, she was informed that she had lost. The incident almost started a riot. Kearney was suspended from school for inciting this "almost" riot. When school officials realized that she was not responsible, she was given a citizenship award for her character.

Kearney's ambition was driven by the feeling that there had to be more to life than what she was being offered. In an environment of violence and theft, Kearney's love of reading led her to steal books to enrich her dreams. In fact, she has kept some of those books as a reminder of her roots. Kearney loved to read about people who were empowering. She consumed vast amounts of poetry and African American literature. She read Langston Hughes, James Baldwin, and similar authors; she disliked books in which "we didn't come out all right in the end."

Kearney feels she has always been an activist for "understanding the power of our voice, our presence, and our person." Yet she also learned to adapt to the various environments in which she found herself. In her own words, she felt she was "destined to be more" than what her immediate circumstances had in store. Though she didn't have a specific plan or vision, she always knew that there was "more."

Kearney said the greatest lesson she learned was one that played out in front of here every day: "When you grow up around a lot of cursing and fighting and cheating and manipulating and get to see the negative impact of that, it teaches you to be respectful of other people's feelings and how those things negatively impact their lives." Kearney said she has always had this intuitive ability to feel what other people were feeling, including their pain.

When asked what advice she would give to young people, she admits, somewhat surprisingly, that she does not believe advice is effective in changing the lives of youth. She believes that young people, instead of trying to follow advice, should learn from the wisdom passed on from their elders. She added, "We must teach and embrace the philosophy of love of our neighbors and love of self." Kearney suggests "that there has to be a shift of focus, of consciousness, and of spirit." She believes that once this shift takes place, we won't have to advise young people on how to change. Instead, we have to create an environment in which young people become forward thinkers so that they can see how hastily made decisions can affect their lives.

According to Kearney, a "Eureka!" moment came when she was working summers throughout high school. Not only did she gain a healthy respect for hard work, but those experiences also reassured her that no matter what happened, she knew how to work hard and could always earn a living.

Soon after, Kearney transferred from Hillsborough Community College in Florida to pursue a degree in social work at Auburn University, where she also became a two-time all-American sprinter. Although she did not grow up wanting to coach, she realized that her education had prepared her to work with student-athletes. Her ambition was to "do something to impact people's lives."

After earning her degree, Kearney moved to California to live with her sister; she worked three jobs and saved money to either purchase a car or move out. Not much later, her junior college coach encouraged her to attend graduate school. Her credentials as an all-American runner led her to a job as a graduate assistant track coach at Indiana State University.

Upon graduation in 1981, Kearney landed her first coaching job, at Toledo University. After helping the women's track team break twenty-five school records during her time there, Kearney was offered an assistant coaching job at the University of Tennessee, where she was the top assistant for the national powerhouse from 1984 to 1986. During her tenure there, Tennessee finished in the top four in nearly every indoor and outdoor national contest; six of her athletes captured national titles, and a dozen earned all-American honors.

With growing success came more attention, and the University of Florida made Kearney the school's youngest head coach ever in any sport in 1988. She would go on to lead one of the top track programs in the country for five years. Kearney led Florida to three Southeastern Conference championships, along with an NCAA indoor championship. For her coaching success, Kearney was named the 1992 NCAA Indoor and Outdoor Coach of the Year. In leading Florida to the 1992 NCAA indoor championship, Kearney became the first African American female head coach to accomplish the feat, and just the second black head coach (after Georgetown's John Thompson, who led a team to the NCAA men's basketball title in 1984) to lead a team to a national title in college sports' top division.

In 1992, while leading Florida to a second-place finish at the NCAA outdoor championships in Austin, Texas, Kearney caught the eye of Jody Conradt, then the University of Texas's women's athletic director and a legendary women's basketball coach. Kearney was offered the head-coaching job at Texas, where she has now been for sixteen years.

For a woman who didn't aspire to become a track coach until she actually became one, Kearney has amassed an impressive record. Since taking over at Texas, Kearney has led Texas to six NCAA titles and nineteen conference championships; for her accomplishments, she has been honored as the national coach of the year four times, district coach of the year nine times, and conference coach of the year fourteen times. And those are only her honors at Texas. Overall, Kearney has thirty-five coach of the year honors; her teams have had thirty national top ten finishes, including six NCAA championship titles, and have won twenty-one conference titles; and her runners have accumulated thirty-one individual and eighteen relay national titles.

Kearney attributes her success to her passion for people and her natural instinct to create a win-win situation. As she put it, "I'm going to benefit, but I'm going to make sure everyone around me benefits also." Kearney believes that this ability to help everyone win has been more important to her success than any technical knowledge she has acquired.

In 2002, Kearney was paralyzed in an auto accident that also took the life of one of her best friends. Many people thought her career was at an end, but the resilience she had developed as a youngster helped her overcome the odds and walk again. She has continued to coach her team and build on its successes, further proving her to be the epitome of resiliency.

Two years later, Kearney was inducted into the International Women's Sports Hall of Fame and later received the Giant Steps Award and the Gary Bridwell Courage Award, given by the Dallas All Sports Association, for her tenacious and ongoing battle to overcome the injuries she sustained in the accident.

Perhaps the next edition of the dictionary will show Kearney's picture next to the word *resilient*.

Part Three

HOW THEY DO IT

CHAPTER 30

Qualities of Real Role Models

The people chronicled in this book are not similar in all regards. In fact, you may have noticed the many differences among them. Some are men and some are women. Some grew up with dreams of becoming the next Dr. King, and some grew up with dreams of becoming the next Dr. J.

Still, there are even subtler differences. Some were raised by both mom and dad, some by one parent, and some by grandparents. Similarly, some grew up in middle-class homes, whereas others were less fortunate. Many became the first person in their families to graduate from college, regardless of socioeconomic status. Likewise, some spent their childhood years in suburbs or near smaller cities, like Beaumont, Texas, or Richmond, Virginia, while others grew up in inner cities, places like LA's Compton, hometown of rap legend Dr. Dre, or New York's Bed-Stuy neighborhood, where Jay-Z lived the street tales he recounts in his lyrics. A commonality: they all realized they could make their own lives better through hard work and persistence.

But it is not just their childhoods that separate them; they also have a diverse set of interests and professional highlights. There is Bernard Muir, who saw his Georgetown Hoyas make college basketball's Final Four thanks to his behind-the-scenes handiwork. And there is Leonard Pitts, Jr., a Pulitzer Prize–winning journalist whose 9/11-inspired column helped us mourn one of the greatest tragedies in American history.

Some of the people chronicled here, like Dr. Tim George and Tracie Hall, have used their education to improve the lives of others. Then there are people like Ed Stewart and Lynn Tyson, who have been recognized as being among the best in their fields largely because of the passion they embody in what they do from nine to five. Then there are those like Rufus Cormier, the award-winning attorney, and Bev Kearney, who became the first black woman to coach a team to an NCAA title; both followed in the footsteps of Jackie Robinson by breaking down barriers in the process.

And while Jackie Robinson, Dr. King, and others helped pave the way for these people to accomplish their goals and become the successes they are today, each of them had less well-known role models as well. Throughout the making of this book, we learned that our profile subjects reached their potential not solely by watching television and reading about celebrities, but by being inspired and motivated by parents, teachers, preachers, and professionals in the community.

For former air force man James McIntyre, a number of officers served as mentors. Reporter Bill Douglas looked to one of the founding members of the National Association of Black Journalists, Acel Moore, to show him a thing or two about journalism. Eric Motley benefited from the model of his grandfather, while Dr. Isiah Warner learned what a PhD meant from a helpful college professor.

What this shows is that regardless of their differences—whether in upbringing or career choice—each looked to their own real role models to help them get where they are today. By looking to their own real role models, these people were able to identify something far more important than the material goods that success can bring. They learned more about success than you ever will from watching *MTV Cribs* or reading an interview in a magazine.

By looking to their own role models, they learned the qualities that make up successful people and people worth admiring and emulating. These qualities include a commitment to hard work, dedication, passion, and a constant desire to learn.

After looking at the people featured in this book and others, we have come to believe that the following qualities are the most important for making someone worthy of being called a real role model. While not all of them may exhibit each attribute, all of them display most of these qualities.

Real role models blaze a path. A real role model is often the first to cross the threshold of a career path or the first to ascend to a particular level or first to achieve a particular status. This doesn't mean that every person has to be the first, but each should have a fervent desire to be the best.

Real role models remain focused on their goals. Real role models don't allow themselves to be sidetracked by unimportant things. Even when they have to redirect their efforts, they realize that a setback is just a setup for a comeback. Willie Miles, Jr., realized that to pursue his goals and spend precious time with his family, he had to leave a well-paying job, return to college, and start his own business. Coach Beverly Kearney had to endure arduous rehabilitation after a tragic auto accident not only to walk again, but also to continue her coaching career.

Life is full of alluring distractions that are easy to succumb to, but real role models are able to look beyond immediate gratification to the lasting satisfaction that comes from achieving long-term goals.

Real role models are willing to do the dirty work. Real role models don't shy away from doing the tough stuff necessary to achieve their goals. They realize that beginners cannot begin at the top. Rising to prominence is not accomplished by filling yourself with hot air, but by engaging in rigorous preparation. When Je'Caryous Johnson put on his first play, he was grossly underpaid. But that play led to another and then to many others for which he was more properly compensated.

Real role models pay their dues. Real role models take the time to learn the skills, get the training, and acquire the experience they need to be successful. Every real role model featured in this book, and anyone else who meets the criteria, speaks freely of the value of education. Education functions in many ways, but the most valuable aspect comes from learning how to learn. No school will teach you everything you need to know, but being immersed in a learning environment will help you realize how you learn. Embrace your learning style and use it to absorb the knowledge you need to become a success. Whether you are an athlete studying film of your favorite pro team or an artist reading books on various techniques, learning and paying your dues through practice and patience will establish a true foundation for success.

Real role models remember where they came from. We are given some choices about where we are headed, but we can't change where we came from. All the real role models featured in this book came from humble beginnings, but they are not ashamed of them. Most of these successful people recognize that the tough environments they grew up in have had a positive impact on their present success. We are all products of our past. Our past molds our understanding of the present and our future. We don't remain in the past, but if our past is filled with valuable life lessons, even unpleasant ones, we can use those lessons to positively shape our future. Coming from a less than ideal past can help us realize just how far we have come and how blessed we are.

Real role models leave the door open for others. Real role models don't have a "I got mine, now you get yours" attitude. They actively seek to reach back and help others achieve their goals. Real role models often go out of their way to mentor, guide, and nurture others in their quest to attain success. Though it is said that our country was built on self-reliance and individualism, much of black culture is built on the concepts of community and interdependence. Anyone with the faintest knowledge of black history realizes the struggles we have endured from slavery, Jim Crow, and the civil rights movement. We all should feel a sense of debt to those who suffered for the freedom and opportunity we have today. To refuse to look back and reach back is a great insult to our past. That is why instead of retiring and enjoying the riches his talents had brought him, people like Horace Allen used their abilities to create opportunities for others. Allen realized that someone opened the door for him, and so he now holds the door open for many others to come through.

Real role models pave the way. Though these real role models had to overcome considerable obstacles to get where they are, they strive to make the path easier to travel for the next person. Real role models have strong shoulders and allow others stand on them. While they may not provide handouts, they will gladly give a hand up.

There are hundreds of people we could have interviewed and written about in this book. But to have interviewed them all would have gone against what is most important in identifying real role models. We do not intend to say, "These are all the real role models in the black community." Instead, we want to say that although they may not all come from the same place or do the same thing for a living, they share the most important qualities that you should aspire to have yourself.

CHAPTER 31

Self-Esteem Is Not Self-Taught

The people featured in these pages have, perhaps more than any other quality, the self-esteem necessary to travel lesser-known routes to success for black Americans. While many of their classmates and childhood friends tried the bumpy road to possible success in the NBA or on the equivalent of today's BET's *106 & Park*, the people we have written about took the highway.

The highway, though, is not a well-traveled path for many black students. Unlike their white counterparts, millions of black students try to take the bumpier path because they believe MVPs and Grammys are better goals than PhDs and law degrees. Unfortunately, when you see those star athletes or entertainers on TV or read their rags-to-riches stories in magazines, you don't hear much about the role education played in getting them to where they are today, or much about the people who helped them find their way. Sometimes it is as if the media wants us to believe these people pulled themselves out of the ghetto or up from poverty with no support from parents, teachers, or mentors. That couldn't be further from the truth.

Like money, self-esteem doesn't grow on trees. However, unlike money, self-esteem can't be taken away once you have it. Only you can control what you think about yourself or your potential. Each of these real role models gained the self-esteem to reach their goals not only by doing well in school, but also by realizing that getting an education would do more for them than anything else—including football practice or popularity—in their young lives.

Real role models acknowledge the importance of education and the contributions others have made to their lives. By recognizing the role played by education in their success, they prove that self-esteem isn't about being your own source of inspiration and motivation, nor is it about practicing alone on a basketball court for hours on end to perfect a jump shot or looking in the mirror and telling yourself that you'll be famous someday. It is about getting on the highway and giving yourself the best chance to succeed.

It is crucial that we say something very important here: we are not opposed to pro athletes or entertainers being role models. Believe us when we say, "We're not haters!" Though our goal with this book is to recognize the contributions and examples of real role models outside the realms of professional sports and entertainment, we realize that there are real role models in those fields as well.

There are many athletes and entertainers who volunteer their time and money for very good causes. Many of these young men and women also conduct themselves in ways that qualify them as real role models. Although young black athletes are often stereotyped as selfish, egotistical, and overpaid, it does not mean that all or most of them fit that description.

And when famous athletes or entertainers do volunteer work or provide financial support to worthy causes, the media is often nowhere to be found. We understand that many good works go unrecognized because the athletes or entertainers do not want to call attention to their good works and neither do the negatively motivated media. If Kobe Bryant runs a youth camp or Tim Duncan provides scholarships for underprivileged children, most would barely notice, but if either were arrested—as was the case for Bryant—it would be national headline news.

Even though the media is unlikely to share positive stories as frequently as negative ones, athletes and entertainers are frequently heralded as role models within the black community. And to be honest, most times this is not because they have the qualities of a real role model. Often it is only after an athlete or entertainer ends up on the front page for misbehavior or bad judgment that we begin reconsidering whether that person should have been called a role model in the first place.

In a way, this seems to be our own "innocent until proven guilty" system for designating black role models. And as we stated at the outset of this book, there have been plenty of guilty verdicts lately, including those for Michael Vick, who landed in prison for dog fighting, and Marion Jones, who had her Olympic gold medals taken away after admitting to steroid use and lying to federal officials.

So why is it that athletes and entertainers are often championed as role models for black youth? It seems the answer has a lot to do with self-esteem. During our adolescent years, many of us look for something—anything, it seems—to identify with in order to help us figure out who we are and what we will become. This is especially true for those who grow up, as we did, underprivileged and without many positive things to identify with inside our communities and homes. We look to television and movies, rap magazines and local sports figures, video games and music videos.

Similarly, too many young blacks, both today and when we were growing up, look to bad role models, like drug dealers, gang members, and other negative influences, because those people have status in the neighborhood or community. Thanks to their status, gained through either notoriety or money, they are seen as sources of guidance and empowerment. What these influencers often forget to tell their young followers is that crime is no lasting or meaningful path to self-esteem and success. Instead, it brings young black people down to a level where education is not valued, goals are not reached, and lives are lost.

For far too many blacks, even if they don't look to drug dealers or gang members as role models, they turn to athletes or entertainers. There are many reasons for this. One has to do with popularity. For example, in too many of our inner-city or underfunded high schools, the students who play on the basketball team or sing in the chorus are far more popular than those who write for the school newspaper or are on the science team. Thus, black children are being told that it is more appropriate to use their energy on athletic or musical pursuits than on academic ones. This message runs in stark contrast to the one that helped make the people in this book successful.

But there is no BET program to showcase the homes and cars of wealthy and successful black doctors, nor is there a magazine or Web site to read about all the successful black professors and attorneys—at least nothing that compares to magazines like *XXL* and *Slam*. And because of this, many young people are more likely to say they hope to become athletes or entertainers rather than accountants or educators.

That said, and as the next chapter will discuss, young black people must look to more positive examples, like the people in this book, for inspiration in order to realize the truth: education is the only real ticket to self-esteem and success.

CHAPTER 32

Education

A REAL TICKET TO SUCCESS

Though many black youth see a sports career or a record deal with a major label as the only ticket out of poverty, a quick review of the facts reveals a different story. Thousands more black youth have escaped poverty via education than through the NBA, the NFL, or by recording a platinum-selling album.

For example, in the 1960s and 1970s, many adults in the black community coveted jobs in the post office. But if someone suggested today that in ten years there would be about five job openings at the post office, no one would encourage or even allow their children or students to train for ten years—devoting large portions of their time to learning how to collect, sort, and deliver the mail—for the mere chance to fill one of those five slots. But that is exactly what happens in sports.

Too many young black males, in particular, sacrifice large amounts of time, effort, and pain to the football and basketball gods, only to end their athletic careers before earning a single dollar from all that hard work. Professional sports are the only careers that require you to volunteer your services for a significant portion of your life, including nearly all of your adolescence, for an astronomically small chance of ever achieving gainful employment in the field. Even musicians can earn a dollar or two strumming a guitar or singing on a street corner.

Additionally, skills acquired in sports are not always transferable to other areas of the work world. There aren't many Fortune 500 companies looking for employees with the cutback and blocking skills of a running back or the ball-handling ability of a point guard. While the concepts of teamwork, endurance, and leadership are said to be by-products of participating in sports, they are seldom traits ascribed to black athletes. Just ask Kobe Bryant and Terrell Owens, who, although among the best in their sports, are criticized for being selfish.

Much of this can be attributed to the misplaced priorities of many in the black community and society in general. While a group of athletically gifted young black men can attract as many as 100,000 people to cram into a stadium to watch them play college football on Saturday night, there would be a scarce fraction of that number to watch them walk across the stage to receive their diplomas at the same university on graduation day. While thousands would scream and cheer on a basketball squad at a Friday-night high school game, only a few would show the same enthusiasm if those student-athletes aced a math test on Monday. But when we step back and analyze this situation, for most of these young men, an A on the math test and a college diploma will be much more meaningful (and valuable) to them in the long run. Touchdown passes and monster dunks are soon forgotten, but educational pursuits pay lasting dividends.

It is not just the black community that is guilty of this infraction. A promising young black athlete can easily become the pride and joy of his community even when it is made up largely of white residents. Parents and coaches alike are almost always supportive and encouraging of a young person's athletic performance. These same parents and coaches may not be as encouraging, or sometimes even aware, of the athlete's academic performance. In fact, some black student-athletes may be labeled as "acting white" when they achieve academically. Again, the message is that performing well in sports, not education, is the only thing you need in order to succeed in life.

A successful sports team can bring a community together, and if a black athlete is an important part of the team, he gains acceptance that may not be present outside the sports environment. In this often repeated scenario, the athlete's academic progress, outside of remaining eligible to play, is seldom encouraged. The story of the star football player who made it all the way to the NFL without learning to read or write is not that different from what happens to thousands of young black men, only most of them never make it to the pros or collect the millions that come with it.

What we want to tell young black men and women is that while sports can provide valuable lessons and skills, they pale in comparison to the benefits of an education. As told by the real role models themselves, here are some of the key benefits to relying on a good education as a foundation for success:

A good education builds confidence. A good education gives you the confidence to perform better in everything you do from that day on. For example, being the first person in your family to graduate from high school can give you the confidence to attend college.

A good education can be shared. A good education doesn't end with you; if you know something, you can share it with others. For example, being good at math may mean that you can be a financial planner or an engineer.

A good education earns respect. While talent alone will get you pretty far in some fields, a good education can earns you the respect to advance more quickly toward your goals and be in a position to teach and train others.

A good education lasts a lifetime. Athletic skills may come and go, but an education can last a lifetime. By continually building upon your educational foundation, you can constantly become more skilled and advanced in your chosen profession or field.

Every person featured in this book has relied heavily on their education to get where they are today. Eric Motley went from PhD to being a special assistant to the president. Bernard Muir draws upon both his college-basketball days and his Ivy League degree to lead Georgetown's athletic department. In total, among the people we profile there are a couple of law degrees, a couple of PhD holders, a few master's degree holders, and three who went to medical school.

These real role models prove that while talented people come and go, and skills can be learned and lost, an education has roots so deep it can support a tree of a person. A tree with branches so far and wide they can help us reach up toward every goal and every aspiration worth having. This tree also has roots so deep they form the foundation that provides the stability not only to withstand life's storms, but also to support others.

CHAPTER 33

Being a Real Role Model

If you understand why education is the only real ticket to success and if you have high self-esteem, you're already halfway to being a real role model. The other half of the job is to follow through.

There are fake, or unreal, role models everywhere. It is a sad truth that some of these live in our own homes. Or maybe they live in our communities, sitting on street corners and waiting for the chance to give false hope about the drug game or shoot down your dreams of making something of yourself by getting an education. On occasion, you may even find one teaching in your school or coaching your team, encouraging you to focus on only what you're good at—you know, like basketball or choir.

But that doesn't mean there aren't real role models around us. Behind or beside us. And sometimes within us. All you have to do is follow through. Following through is a combination of three things:

Working hard to achieve your goals. Plenty of people try to get by in this world on talent alone, but only an ethic of hard work can be sustained for a lifetime. Following through means always giving the maximum effort to accomplish what you set out to do.

Never losing passion for what you do. While fame and fortune lead some to lose the drive and energy they had for achieving their goals as youth, following through means staying passionate about your life's work even after you've made it to the top.

Doing the right thing. While no one is perfect and we all make bad decisions from time to time, doing the right thing—by yourself, by the people who are important to you, and by those who look up to you—means you are following through on your responsibility as a real role model.

While many people are heralded as role models within the black community, a much smaller number follow through in these three aspects. Even with these three aspects, however, following through is not an easy concept to understand completely. You see, every person profiled in this book has high self-esteem. They have to, otherwise they would never have risen to their current positions or made it out of poverty-stricken, crime-ridden places like Compton, California, as Tracie Hall did, or into the White House, as Eric Motley did.

All of these people also fully understood the importance of a good education for getting them to the places they could have only imagined as teenagers. Dr. Tim George, for example, went through years of college and then medical school to become a surgeon. And even after that, he had more years as a resident, earning minimal wages to save lives and pay his dues.

And it should not be forgotten that each of the real role models here looked to those before them for counsel and guidance and inspiration. Melody Barnes, to name one, looked to Ella Baker, the great civil rights voice, to see what was possible for a young black woman. Similarly, James McIntyre looked to a fellow military man, General Colin Powell, for an idea of what a black man in a uniform could do for his country.

Still, even with those pieces, it took follow-through. And real role models, as each person here deserves to be called, make it look easy. In fact, these people are not all that different from Michael Jordan, whose own follow-through made gliding through the air and switching the ball in his hands on the way to the hoop look easy. Only these people have received no fame or fortune, at least nothing comparable to Jordan's, for their accomplishments.

But recognition and revenue are not the true pursuits of real role models. Instead, these people use their know-how, passion, and skills to pursue a sense of purpose that all real role models share. They may all have different educational backgrounds and upbringings and professions and personal interests, but they share a desire—we learned while making this book—to improve on they came from or where they are. They seek to follow through on what too many of their peers, from grade school to graduate school, failed to.

They follow through on the other half of being a real role model, which is to do right by the people who helped them get where they are today, and to help others follow in their footsteps. Each of them has his or her own methods, but all have served, and continue to serve, in mentor or advisory roles for others, especially young people. They use their life lessons as a backdrop for their advice, and rely on their success as their credentials, but most importantly, they pull from a deep-rooted sense of purpose to help others make something of themselves.

They teach science, they give financial advice, they put on shows, they coach teams, they lead organizations, they make art, and they run businesses. More significantly, they continually learn, they consistently succeed, and they constantly share their knowledge and wisdom with others—much like the elders during the civil rights movement and the elders on southern plantations and the elders in African tribes.

Half of being a real role model is to *know* what matters. By reading this book, we hope, you know now exactly what that is. The other half of being a real role model is to *do* what matters. Only you can figure out what that is.

CHAPTER 34

Final Thoughts

Real Role Models was a challenging yet fulfilling endeavor for Louis and me. The challenge was how two authors—one in Austin, Texas, and the other in Washington, D.C.—could stay on the same page throughout the making of a book. The fulfillment came in being able to do just that. Louis and I wanted to conclude the book by sharing some final thoughts on the final result.

LOUIS

This is probably the most important thing I have ever done. It is an opportunity to reach many more people than I would with an article in an academic journal. Not a lot of people have successful figures around them, so this book is meant to let young people know that there is hope and that they can be anything. I think too many people tell kids, "You can be anything," but then don't show them the way. It is a hollow thing to say if there is no follow-through. It is not easy for kids to be ambitious; they have a lot to deal with. But this book shows that if you come from humble beginnings and go on to excel, your success drives you not just to get to a certain point, but to go forward from there, even when you have already reach a satisfying level of success. I hope that people will take this book and fill in the middle and show the concrete steps or draw a road map for success in a language that young people will respond to.

JOAH

Whenever I identify the intended audience for this book, I always start by saying that this is a book made for my fourteen- or sixteen- or even eighteen-year-old self. I would have loved to know about people like this when I was going through high school and college. So many black kids grow up with the idea that role models are the people they see on TV. And even though I admire people like Will Smith and Jay-Z, their stories are not unique to actors and rappers. I hope this book shows that people from places like West Philadelphia and Brooklyn become doctors, engineers, and teachers. You don't have to want to be famous to want to be considered a success. Everyone has a definition of success, but the shared attributes among the people in this book should be qualities we should encourage all young people to aspire to have for themselves.

About the Authors

JOAH SPEARMAN is the youngest of three boys raised by a single mother. He earned more than two dozen academic and nonprofit scholarships to attend the University of Texas at Austin, becoming, in 2005, the first person in his immediate family to receive a four-year college degree.

While at Texas, Joah became the first black member of one of Delta Sigma Phi's oldest chapters, where he was honored as "Best New Member." Also, to benefit a local children's hospital, Joah helped establish an event that has raised more than $100,000 in just five years. For his involvement in local and statewide March of Dimes events, Joah was honored with the organization's national scholarship in 2001.

While attending college full-time, Joah worked in communications for the University of Texas, Motorola, and Southwest Airlines. Just days after Hurricane Katrina, Joah moved to Washington, D.C., to serve as principal speechwriter for David Paulison, the newly appointed director of FEMA.

Currently, Joah lives in Austin, Texas, where he consults with companies and nonprofits on social media and is working on a book about the city's live music scene. He is an avid runner; a student of pop culture, sports, and entertainment; and a supporter of the Institute for Responsible Citizenship, an organization that brings talented black male college students to D.C.

LOUIS HARRISON, JR., PhD, is an associate professor in the Department of Curriculum and Instruction in the College of Education and the Center for African and African-American Studies at the University of Texas at Austin. He also supports the Texas Longhorns, which, in various sports, are ranked among the leading college athletic programs in the nation.

Previously, Louis spent twelve years at Louisiana State University. While there, he received several honors, including the Exemplary Models of Administrative Leadership Award from the American Association of University Administrators in 2006, and was recognized by the LSU seniors as a "Favorite Faculty Member."

Before serving as a professor at LSU and the University of Southwestern Louisiana, Louis served for seven years as a teacher and coach in Louisiana's Jefferson Parish School District. Louis has served on the boards of a number of national organizations as well as on the editorial boards of professional journals.

A native of New Orleans, Louis earned both his bachelor's and master's in education from the University of New Orleans and his PhD in kinesiology pedagogy from LSU.